SETH

ON DEATH

AND

THE AFTERLIFE

-- An Experiential Guide --

Copyright © 2014 by Mark Allen Frost

First Edition

Seth Returns Publishing

Editorial: Mark Frost

Cover Art, Design, Typography & Layout:

Mark Frost

Library of Congress Control Number: 2014912986

ISBN 13: 9780974058658

ISBN 10: 0974058653

Dedicated to my parents, Joy and Allen.

I am grateful for the Love, the life

and the Lessons that continue.

CONTENTS

Introduction by Mark

Hello everybody. Welcome to the new book. The idea for a book on death and the afterlife first came up, back when we were putting the 911 book together with Seth. It seemed like a good idea at the time. Seth would tell us, from his perspective, what it was like in the non-physical world. The idea of death then was pretty foreign to me, almost abstract. I had not been touched by death in many years. In my ignorance, I thought a Death Book would be interesting and adventurous. But I was so busy at the time, with graduate school, with a homelife, and with the Seth project, that I was forced to put it on the back burner. It stayed on the back burner for twelve years.

When my father died in 2009 I grieved and I was informed by Seth about what was going on with my father and his Transition. I appreciated Seth's unconventional view. My mother passed away in 2013, and again Seth counseled me on what was occuring with my mother during and after her Transition.

On my trip to India in May of 2014 I felt the urgency and the necessity of coming to terms with the death of my parents, by telling others what I had learned from Seth about the Transition and the Afterlife. When I returned from India I immediately began to take dictation from Seth for this book. I hope that the reader can take a similar journey through their fears, to consider this fantastic voyage that Seth is describing in his book. It is very, very worthwhile.

When you come across words or phrases that you are not familiar with, turn to the Glossary at the back of the book. There you will find definitions for most of the concepts Seth uses in this book.

When you read the words **Create a Light Trance State**, Seth wants you to use meditation, visualization, self-hypnosis or other relaxation techniques to focus on your inner world.

Introduction by Seth

To understand your Transition and the After-life, you are advised to explore the subject matter bravely. I have sprinkled several Experiments throughout this book, so that you may do your own research within your own consciousness. When I ask that you consider taking a tour of your personal Afterlife with me, this means you will do the Experiments, even though you may have Issues around death and dying. This is what Loving Understanding and Courage is all about, you see. The Scientist of Consciousness moves forward bravely in the exploration of the personal psyche, in spite of the fear of death Issue.

We treat death rather lightly in this teaching of mine. I do not consider this macabre in the least. I propose a pleasant death and an Afterlife of Loving appreciation for yourself and for others. Thus, when I suggest to you that you are already dead, I am not trying to shock you. I am not trying to be sacrilegious. I am simply stating a literal fact of your condition. You ARE already dead, Dear Reader. You ARE forever on the cusp of dying, of ceasing to exist. The cliché that you are a Soul having a human experience is relevant here. This means that you are alive and dead at the same time. You are in your body in the world of the Third Dimension AND you are out of your body in the other dimensions.

During the weeks ahead, as you read this book and conduct your experiments, I suggest that you begin each day by creating Sanctuary. Turn to the Ritual of Sanctuary instructions in the back of the book, and create your Sanctuary as soon as you awaken for the day. Carry this altared state of consciousness with you as you go about your waking activities. You will be happy that you took my advice.

Preface

Dear Reader, we are not anti-religion as we present this theory of mine in this new book. It is not our intention to disrupt nor to defame. We are, however, pro-truth here. We are always looking for "the truth of the matter," as we say. The truth with regards to death and the afterlife, is unfortunately, hidden beneath the dogma of most of the world religions. The Truth has been covered up by intermediaries in the church hierarchies. This is a common practice, as you may know.

Rather than go through an intermediary, we advocate a direct experience approach, here in this book. This means that the reader is encouraged to have an open mind and an open heart. These two centers must be wide open, in order for the truth to be perceived. The head and the heart. Do you understand? What I ask is that you attempt to be open to the direct experience approach and allow your own inner guidance, what you may call your Source or your Intuition, to assist you in determining what is of value, what is true, what resonates with you personally.

Now, whatever religious beliefs you may hold, as to what occurs after death, we honor that as your personal truth. What we offer you in this book is an alternative storyline.

This manuscript is based upon the basic tenets of my theory of Reality Creation. I have taught this theory in books, in workshops and in telephone and face-to-face sessions with my students. It is a very unusual story, this theory of life and death I am about to present to you. In this theory I make use of powerful Essential Metaphors. Indeed all of my concepts that I will discuss in these pages are metaphors, Dear Reader. The concepts of separate Dimensions, Soul Identity, Inner Senses, the Personal Reality Field, The Telepathic Network, and the other esoteric sounding words and phrases, are simply metaphors of my creation. With these descriptive and hopefully evocative Essential Metaphors, I strive to reveal the activity of consciousness becoming realities. In so doing, I hope to reveal YOU to yourself.

Chapter 1
The Dimensions of Reality

"Your Home Dimension is your home away from home. It is where you go in between lives."

A Theory of Creation

This is a book on death, but to begin this story we must begin with life, with the inception of life into your system. Imagine, then, that you are not yet physically embodied as you are now, but simply an impulse of potential life. You exist in potential within the Primary Creative Gestalt that creates all realities. I refer to this energy body as All That Is. This is how it begins. The you that you are, that you know as you, did exist first within All That Is and was then expressed in an energy body that you know as a star within a star system. This extra-dimensional system included other bodies that you call planets, moons and the ephemera of cosmic stuff you know as comets and other material.

SETH

You may think of these stars in the sky as inhospitable, perhaps, for you have been told that they cannot support life. My suggestion to you now, is to change your focus a bit, and see them from the perspective of your ancient ancestors. The view of the original peoples of your Earth was that the skies were the origins of all life, including human life. It was home. Now in this moment, you have it within you, in your DNA code, to once again perceive through these lenses of perception that your ancestors used as a matter of course. In my books I refer to them as the Inner Senses.

The Inner Senses

Through this perspective, the stars, the planets, the comets are perceived as bodies of light energy vibrating at different frequencies. Through these same senses, your physical body, the people in front of you, all of the Reality Constructs that compose your Personal Reality Field, also appear as bodies of light energy, each vibrating at a signature frequency, one that identifies it for what it is. As you use your Inner Sense of sight, for example you may begin to see a slight auric corona surrounding the construct, then the body of light phenomenon will become apparent. If you use your Inner Sense of hearing, you may begin to pick up on voices and sounds from the non-physical world.

Death and the Afterlife

Currently, the Inner Senses are used unconsciously. They assist in the creation of your physical senses and your perceived realities. However, as you awaken you begin to use them consciously. The Inner Senses are also used in the Afterlife. If you are spiritually minded, you might say that they are the senses of your Soul. When you first take the journey from your Star System into physical form, before you place your energy within the body of the baby, you are using the Inner Senses to "look into" the life you are considering. You are thus able to get a sense of what is in store for you, in a very, very general way, should you decide to experience the proposed life.

Soul Contract

The Soul Contract is the broad plan that you agree to, before you move into another life in a human body. You receive a great deal of guidance in creating this Soul Contract. We will have more to say about your Guides in later chapters. For now consider this: You have seen the future, somewhat, through the Inner Senses, and you agree to experience, again, in a very general way, a life of Issues. Your Issues present particular challenges to your development. You are challenged to face your problems and learn your Lessons by resolving them.

SETH

Issues and Lessons

For example: Suppose you are an angry person. You have been that way since you were quite young. The tendency for you is to react with anger to the ordinary frustrations of living. You are now an adult and your anger is beginning to get you in trouble, with your family, with your employer, with your friends. It suddenly becomes apparent to you, in a flash of insight - I am being humorous here - that you may have an anger Issue. You are only now discovering what your family, your employer and your friends have always known. In this momentary awakening, your Ego/Intellect has diminished, and your Soul has come through. You are ready to address your Issue. Perhaps you will go to Anger Management Classes. Perhaps you will learn how to meditate. By addressing your Issue actively, you are learning your Lesson.

However, all of you have free-will in the Third Dimension. Thus, we have the very common phenomenon of humans denying their Issues and avoiding their Lessons altogether. This cycle of reincarnation that sees the Soul taking human form lifetime after lifetime, moving into physical life and then transitioning into the non-physical dimensions, this is what I refer to as the Simultaneous Lives.

Death and the Afterlife

Simultaneous Lives

You create your reality, Dear Reader. What you think of, what you imagine, what you believe becomes real. With your consciousness, you combine the elements of creation to construct your world. These elements of creation I call Consciousness Units, or CU's. They are the building blocks of all realities in the physical and the non-physical dimensions. They are holographic and telepathic in nature. They provide the structural support for the Telepathic Network that connects YOU to all of humanity. The CU's behave in distinct ways that provide the electro-magnetic energy for the creation of Reality Constructs of infinite variety; constructs including YOU and everything you see in front of you in your Personal Reality Field.

See When You Walk Across the Room at the back of the book.

Multi-dimensional Existence

Now you exist currently in the Third Dimension, on the physical plane. But just beyond this Earthly domain is your Home Dimension. The Home Dimension is your home away from home. It is where you go in between lives. This etheric locale exists outside of time and space as you understand these terms. Beyond that are the Fifth and the Sixth Dimensions. They are the planes within which The Council, the Spiritual Hierarchy and the various Guides function. We will cover the non-physical beings in a later chapter.

In these descriptions I use the word dimension for the sake of convenience, for you are quite probably familiar with the word, as a reader of metaphysical literature. I am attempting to draw distinctions between the planes of existence, so that you may understand the different activities that take place there. Yet, all of these dimensional planes I speak of in my books are not separate at all. They are all, in fact, ONE. They all take up the same "space" in front of you and around you. They are all made of the same CU's that compose your physical body and the Reality Constructs that populate your Personal Reality Field.

I have referred to the dimensions as being related in a holographic fashion, meaning, in their entirety, each within all of the other dimensions. I have also referred to the dimensions of existence as nested realities, each separate dimension nested within the other. The Russian doll comparison works here also, I believe. The large Russian doll is opened to reveal a slightly smaller doll within it. That doll is opened to reveal a slightly smaller doll within it also, and so on. The difference being, with the multidimensional example, the dolls would extend infinitely both within and without. Do you see?

Dimensions of Consciousness

All of the dimensions represent the creative output of Evolutionary Consciousness. With regards to All That Is, anything that can happen does indeed happen within a dimension in some system of reality and continues to evolve according to the "rules" of that system. There are an infinite number of systems and an infinite number of dimensions. There are Dimensions of Love where negative emotion is not permitted. There are Dimensions where the core assumptions you enjoy on Earth, that act to create a stable reality, are absent. For example: On Earth you have rules governing your physical reality, such as gravity and cause-and-effect. In other systems, gravity and cause-and-effect are not operative. These dimensions would appear quite alien to you if you were to unexpectedly find yourself in the middle of one. This does occur in the dream state for some people, when they accidentally tune-in to that frequency. Those undergoing the "psychotic reaction," are actually experiencing a dimensional bleedthrough into the negative or Nightmare Dimensions.

SETH

There are Hellish Dimensions. These Gestalts of Consciousness are energized by the hateful thoughts, images, and emotions of humans over the generations. Of course, there exist also the Paradisiacal Dimensions, created through the adoration and Loving thought energy of humans in prayer. My point is this: As a creative thinking human, you give birth to dimensions unknown to you, with every energized thought or empowered image you entertain within your consciousness. You create worlds, then, just by thinking about them or fantasizing about them. These worlds of probability continue on and develop in their own ways from their inception. These created dimensions of reality are available to you now, in this moment, and they will be available to you also after you make your Transition.

Holographic and Telepathic
All of your lives co-exist, one within the other, including your original existences within the Star Systems, including your Simultaneous Lives, including your Afterlife existences within your Home Dimension. My theory of Simultaneous Time allows for this relationship of the current you, with all of the other you's that exist throughout perceived time.

Death and the Afterlife

Then, if you comprehend this theory somewhat, you may take advantage of it by experimenting with your perceptions as you read this book. For example: When I say that you may multitask, by enjoying a moment of time within another life, or within the Home Dimension, or within a Star System, even as you read this book, that is Simultaneous Time you are experiencing, when you do get some effects.

Dear Reader, you are composed of the Consciousness Units that are telepathic and holographic. This means that YOU are telepathic and holographic. YOU are able to exist in multiple lives. YOU are able to bridge the Third and the Home Dimensions and others with your consciousness.

Scientist of Consciousness

I have just presented you with some of the key concepts I use to teach my theory of Reality Creation to my students. Now I suggest you put the material to use by participating in some experimentation within your Personal Reality Field. As the researcher studying your own psyche, you may adopt the role of Scientist of Consciousness. This is a term I first coined in my second book since my return to publishing. A Scientist of Consciousness utilizes their powerful Inner Senses to explore the multidimensional realities of consciousness. As you conduct the experiments, remember to document in some form, the outcomes. These Findings will serve you in creating your own personal storyline regarding this matter of Death and the Afterlife.

End of Chapter Experiments

Experiment: Using the Inner Senses
In this first experiment of the book, you will become acquainted with the Inner Senses. The Inner Senses are the originators of the sensory experiences of the physical senses. The Inner Senses help to create your perceived reality.

Create a Light Trance State

So I would ask you to perhaps close your eyes as you enjoy this Light Trance State, and begin to conceive of the Inner Sense of sight. You know what your physical sense of sight provides for you. You experience visual information, the sights of your Personal Reality. With your eyes closed, imagine where your physical sight originates. As you get a sense of this, allow your consciousness to drift, with the Intention to experience inner visionary material. When you receive some visual information, whether flashes of light or complete clear images, congratulate yourself. Attempt to keep yourself at that depth of Trance in which you experienced success. Have an Intention to experience the Inner Sense of hearing. Anticipate having success. When you experience some success, as in hearing faint sounds, talking or music, congratulate yourself. Give yourself the suggestion that you will remember the Feeling-Tones experienced in the experiment. When you are ready, slowly return to surface awareness.

Findings: Document your Findings in some way for future reference.

Experiment: Sense Your Star Origins
You are from a Star System that is many light years away from Earth, in terms of distance. However, with these techniques of experimentation, you may easily visit your birth home instantly.

Create a Light Trance State

Now close your eyes and consider the information I provided for you earlier. I stated that you exist in the Third Dimension, but that you have immediate access to all of the other dimensions, by virtue of these connective elements, the Consciousness Units. This is your reasoning, then, as an adult. However, as a child, perhaps you were able to easily remember that you were from the stars. Return to those days now, for just a few moments. Do you

SETH

see? It makes perfect sense when you have the correct perspective, the right instruments for viewing, these Inner Senses. Many of my students have identified the Sirius and the Arcturus Star Complexes as their Star Origins. When you feel you have received sufficient data, return to surface awareness.

Findings: Document your Findings in your preferred medium.

Experiment: Sense Your Home Dimension

My students often ask me, "What does it feel like to be in the Home Dimension." I sometimes turn the tables on them by asking, "Perhaps you can tell <u>me</u> how it feels, for you are there now. You are in your Home Dimension NOW, even as you sit here in this lecture hall asking me this question." In this Experiment, you may have an opportunity to discover the truth of my statement. Now you will learn a great deal more about the Home Dimension in the following chapters. For now, I would like you to consider this idea, that you ARE there now, just as surely as you ARE here in your physical body in the Third Dimension. The Home Dimension is familiar to you. This exercise is easy to do. It should take you only about twenty minutes.

Death and the Afterlife

Create a Light Trance State

Relax, close your eyes, and consider those times in your life when you are in touch with your Source. At these times, it is almost as though you are downloading information into your consciousness. There is a comforting energy that comes upon you at these times. Often, it seems as though someone is trying to tell you something, something important. You may have flashes of images, faces of people you recognize but do not know. There may be some religious symbolism here for you to recognize. If you find something that is disagreeable to you, you simply let it pass and continue exploring. When you feel as though you have a sense of having visited your Home Dimension, slowly return to surface awareness.

Findings: Document your Findings.

A Personal Note

At times, as you conduct your experiments, you may be inclined to pause and chuckle to yourself at the outrageous claims I make in the text. That is normal. I encourage you to enjoy frequent moments of Good Humor. So take your breaks. Consider how unbelievable the subject matter is. And then return to the book.

Chapter 2
A Death in the Soul Family

"The arrangements are made on the Etheric Levels, as we say, in the dream state, in the so-called astral realms".

Soul Family Theory

Over the years I have simplified my Teaching to clarify what I mean by the word Soul. From my perspective, you-the-reader have a unique Soul Identity. This uniqueness is apparent in the personalities of all of your lives that you live throughout time. Yet, where I once referred to these unique features as representing your connections to various Families of Consciousness, Entities and Over Souls, I now speak of your place within a single Soul Family collective that manifests differently in each of your reincarnational lives.

Each of you belongs to a Soul Family that includes members of your genetic family, your adoptive family, your friends and extended family, and each person who is in your life to learn

SETH

their Lessons with you. Over time, over the generations, over the millennia, beginning from your Star Origins, you and your Soul Family members interact, form families, address your Issues and learn your Lessons in relationships of all kinds.

For Example: Now in this lifetime you may be the daughter of a mother and father, and the sister of a brother. However, in a past life, in a different configuration of the same Soul Family, you are the father, and your wife is your current mother though in a different body, obviously. Other members of your current Soul Family have also incarnated into this past life to adopt different roles in the collective. The Soul Family is this constantly evolving repertory enactment of family roles by the same Souls in different bodies in different timeframes. Do you see?

The Soul Family Gestalt

Now we will discuss the death process as it plays out within the greater Soul Family, what we call the Soul Family Gestalt. This vast collective includes the members of the current Soul Family, and also those representing the Simultaneous Lives of the Soul Family. This is the Soul Family throughout time.

Death and the Afterlife

An impending death sends urgent messages throughout the Telepathic Network of the Soul Family Gestalt. Although the family as a whole decides on the particulars of any one Transition, with management duties assigned to the transitioning member and their Soul Identity, there is no fate involved. All outcomes are reached through the free-will choices of family members. We will talk about the influence of the nonphysical beings, including The Council and others, in a later chapter.

A Transition Strategy

Briefly, once any Soul Family member has suitably fulfilled their obligations with regards to participation in their individual existence AND the Soul Family, a strategy for creating the Transition into the Home Dimension is devised. Normally, this is not consciously constructed. The arrangements are made on the Etheric Levels, as we say, in the dream state, in the so-called astral realms. In this Pre-manifestation Domain each member of the entire Soul Family Gestalt considers the life lived by the potential transitioning member, and asks themselves:

- ❖ Were Lessons learned or avoided?

- ❖ What may be left for other incarnations?

SETH

❖ What of my participation in the life of this Soul Family member?

Each member of the Gestalt considers their part in the life of the potential transitioning member. They question whether their actions or inactions were appropriate or not appropriate in the learning of Lessons. In a sense, you could say that mental "notes" are taken by all on a subconscious level. These notes will be referred to in other incarnations of the Soul Family. But just as notes may be used in only a cursory fashion, as reminders, these notes may be used in other incarnations as simply suggestions of ways to approach interacting with a particular Soul Family member.

No Judgment No Guilt

And there is no judgment, here, with regards to Issues and Lessons being acknowledged or learned. There is no guilt associated with not living up to the expectations of the Soul Contract. Indeed, an Issue unrecognized or a Lesson completely avoided, represents important information for the Soul. This is data that may be used in planning further physical incarnations for the Soul Identity. I will continually remind you throughout this volume of this important fact of existence.

Death and the Afterlife

Now I shall discuss how the common means of death are achieved in your world.

The Means of Death

The Medical Model

In modern times, the tenets of the medical model of healthcare shape the death experience for those patients who find themselves in that system. I have likened the medical establishment to a religious institution. The doctors behave like priests, overseeing the death process. Within this medical model, the beliefs of the patient often coincide with the beliefs of the medical practitioners. The living or dying becomes a collaborative effort. For example: The patient, believing the prognosis of the doctor, and communicating via the Telepathic Network, will dutifully create the necessary supporting symptoms and signs of the malady, and perhaps die on schedule, totally supporting the prognosis.

Chronic Illness

Indeed, it is very common for humans to create a chronic illness subconsciously, react to it as though they are being set upon from without, and then follow through with their own demise, as though they were helpless to do anything about it. This drama of illness and death is usually the result of a collaborative effort between the "victim," their doctors, the hospital and the entire medical and pharmaceutical industries. The reincarnational drama is founded upon cultural mis-perceptions and unhealthy beliefs systems acted out within the Telepathic Network and then in physical reality.

The mis-perceptions involve fears of being contaminated by disease agents that are "everywhere." The germs, bacteria, and deadly diseases are thought to be more powerful than the human capabilities to resist them. These thoughts of weakness and vulnerability compromise the immune system and create a friendly environment in which the contaminating agents may thrive.

I maintain that the chronic illness that leads to death, is often a subconscious strategy used by the "victim" to address personal and Soul Family Issues and Lessons.

For Example: When a Soul Family member succumbs to a disease, while lying in a bed in the local hospital, they are confirming deeply held cultural beliefs about the vulnerability of the individual. When the sons and daughters eventually die of the same malady, they are, in a sense "supporting and validating" the parents and their chosen pathways

Death and the Afterlife

to death. But it is not the genetic predisposition that they inherit from the parents, as much as it is the "sick" belief system they learned from them, that creates the illness and ultimately the deaths.

Now yes, it is true that old age brings death. Yet in many cases where the individual succumbs to disease, long before old age and infirmity have set in, they are acting according to the conditioned programming of the subconscious mind. Again, it is a collaboration with Soul Family members and all of the players. Everyone contributes in the Telepathic Network to support the process.

Accidents

As you know, I espouse an accident free zone in the Third Dimension. There are no accidents, there are only Reality Creation projects carried out by individuals and collectives. Most of human activity is carried out unconsciously and automatically. The subconscious drives most of your reality, then. Having said that, let me comment briefly on what makes an accidental death, from my perspective.

I would identify a fatal accident as a very unfortunate negative reality. Now a negative reality sends out signals to the potential participants before the reality emerges into your dimension.

SETH

The signals act as a type of portending, or preface, if you will, to the probable event. The Feeling-Tones of these ominous communications from the probable future, have negative emotions, such as fear, anger, distress, helplessness attached to them. The human experiencing this communication stream from within their mental environment is being triggered to re-create the negative emotions. It is a warning, in a sense, that tragedy is awaiting this human in the future, if they continue on their path of Reality Creation. The human who is aware of this signaling, may express feelings of despair, anger, being unlucky, and so on.

Now, this person has their own Issues and Lessons that they are learning. And because they create their own reality through the ideas, images, and emotions they are experiencing in the moment, the signaling from the Negative Probable Future event may have the effect of assisting the human in creating the accidental death experience. Rather than interpreting the signaling as a warning and changing their behavior, perhaps because of their Issues, they re-create the Negative State of Consciousness habitually, which then leads to the accident.

A similar portending occurs when a Positive Probable Future event sends back information to the potential experiencer of the event. The communication stream of this signaling is of a positive nature. The person is triggered to re-create positive emotions within their consciousness. They may express feelings of abundance and happiness, that something good is coming their way. They recreate these positive aspects of consciousness habitually, and act to support and create the Positive Reality.

Now of course, these are general descriptions of how unfortunate and happy accidents play out. It is seldom clear-cut and obvious. But I am certain that you have experienced both forms of communication coming from the Probable Future. Again, it is not fate, that someone dies and another experiences a positive event. The "reasons" for all accidents are to be found in the complex interactions of multiple Souls in incarnation.

Suicide

Let me add here to the material I covered in my 911 book on suicide and how it occurs within the individual and the collective consciousness of the Soul Family. Now, it is always about Lessons, here, with this act of suicide. Primarily, it is a group Lesson for the Soul Family, including persons you might not think of as family. For remember, the Soul Family may include the friendly waiter at the local restaurant, the stranger you bump into on the street, and even the co-worker who rubs you the wrong way at work. Soul Family members come together to learn their Lessons as a group.

Now a suicide in the Soul Family is never a surprise. In the Telepathic Network that connects the consciousness of each member to all members of the Soul Family, all is known, all is considered, all plans are made, all secrets are revealed.

And of course, in each case, there are the extenuating circumstances, the reasons, the impulses that lead to the act. These reasons for committing the act highlight and define this final event in the life of the Soul Identity in terms of Value Fulfillment. Usually, the Soul is required to immediately return to the Earth plane, the reason being that the important Lesson of the value of life was not learned completely. Yet there are the obvious exceptions that must be made in these matters, in cases of compromised functioning of the consciousness, in cases of severe mental illness, torture, unbearably painful physical symptoms, and others. It is largely a matter of how thoroughly the Lessons were learned in the life to that point. Also, it may be that the Soul incarnated into the body of the particular human to experience the ending of that life at their

Death and the Afterlife

own hands. It may have been in the Soul Contract, and so is not a Violation.

Please see the sections on the Spiritual Hierarchy and The Council.

Violent Deaths

Those who have incurred violent deaths may be subject to a type of etheric dissociation and dislocation. They become lost within the extra-dimensional planes. The Ego/Intellect suddenly disrupted, loses all bearings and becomes disoriented. In some cases, the consciousness of the transitioning human becomes trapped in an inter-dimensional loop, in which they re-create the death experience over and over. The Ego/Intellect survives the Transition, yet is not functioning properly, for it is still attempting to make Third-Dimensional sense out of a Fourth-Dimensional experience. Often, however, appropriate enactments of suitable After Death scenarios are portrayed by Soul Family members who have made their Transitions and are stabilized in the Home Dimension. (See Chapter Three.) Those Souls that do not receive this support are sometimes identified as ghosts, poltergeists and unruly spirits, as they are sensed in bleedthrough experiences by others still in physical form.

SETH

Murder

You play many roles throughout your reincarnational lives. All That Is seeks out experiences of all types in the search for Value Fulfillment. If you have been murdered in one or more of your lives, the odds are that you have murdered in one or more of your lives. There is no hard and fast rule, however. There is also no "tit for tat," as espoused by some interpreters of the so-called Law of Karma. You are not murdered in one life, BECAUSE you were a murderer in a past life. This does occur, but it is rare, and most certainly not predictable. Free-will is operative in each moment of the life of the human on Earth. However, you will be required to immediately return to the Third Dimension after your death if you have murdered someone. The reasoning here is that if you took another's life, you did not learn the Lesson of the sanctity of life.

This is very similar to the case of the suicide. Therefore, the Soul would necessitate your returning to physical form, to experience similar conditions as the previous life, to give you an opportunity to make better choices and perhaps learn the Lesson.

Dying Young

The subject of dying young was covered in my book **Soul Mate Soul Family**. I will now say a few

Death and the Afterlife

more words about this difficult subject. The question we pondered was this: What are the Lessons for the human who dies as a child and what are the Lessons for the Soul Family? It does seem to be a tragedy, from whatever perspective you look at it. However, I believe we may bring some clarity to the discussion when we look on these events as Lessons, primarily for the child, and secondarily for the Soul Family members who are left to grieve.

All members of the Soul Family Gestalt understand, on a subconscious level, the motives, the reasons, the Lessons involved in a member of the family dying at a young age. But particularly the transitioning young person is aware of the critical role they are playing in the learning of Lessons. These are often Wisdom Lessons, here, in which the wise Old Soul of the child, teaches the younger Souls of the parents, you see. This is very often the case, that the child teaches the parents. And most certainly, the Soul Contracts in these cases stipulate that the human will take an "early out," so to speak. For the parents, and other Soul Family members, the heart opens and is transformed and the Ego/Intellect is diminished. The Soul Evolution of all concerned is furthered.

SETH

Abortion

In the case of abortion, I have answered this question many times, the question being, "When does the Soul enter into the consciousness of the baby?" Again we may easily be trapped in a game of semantics and differing definitions. Let me be blunt, then. The Soul of which I speak is a construct particular to my Teaching, but has obvious similarities to other conceptualizations of the Divine you may have come across in your studies. The Soul is the non-physical counterpart to the physical human body, the personality, and the mentality. The Soul is the spiritual aspect of the human.

There is no specific "time" or moment that the Soul "decides" to impart a fragment of itself to another human consciousness. As usual, it is another collaborative effort between all of the players, past, present and future.

For example, the Soul may wish to experience life in the growing fetus, but may not wish to experience the birth and the succeeding life. It extricates itself, then, prior to the spontaneous abortion or the medical procedure. This is quite common in your system. There is no suffering, you see. The consciousness, the Soul, withdraws its essence from the physical body construct, prior to the imminent destruction of the physical body. This is a rule within your system. The consciousness vacates the physical body before a violent death. It is true for the mouse killed by the cat, as I have stated before in another manuscript. It is true for all living beings.

Effects Within the Other Lives

I am often asked whether a death of one life in the Simultaneous Lives results in or causes a death in other of the lives? The answer is that all of the Simultaneous Lives are affected to some degree when one of the lives comes to an end. The Transition in one life, however, does not <u>cause</u> a death in another of the lives.

As you may know, your current identity is in fact, a type of mix-and-match expression from your greater consciousness. By this I mean, you are constantly selecting from your Simultaneous Lives, the aspects of personality, mood, and essence that you will use to create the next moment of your identity in the Third Dimension. Your identity, then, is an evolving event in linear time, as you spontaneously select the attributes you will portray to others and to yourself as YOU. Now, when one of your Simultaneous Lives makes their Transition, this effectively takes them out of this creative process. They are no longer part of the mix you use to create yourself. You may feel the loss profoundly or you may perceive it as a momentary lapse in consciousness, recover and move on. You have a multitude of reincarnational existences from which to choose your various aspects of identity.

The following will help you to explore in depth the subject matter I have just covered.

End of Chapter Experiments

Experiment: Experience Simultaneous Time
A playful attitude is required for this Experiment.

Create a Light Trance State

Relax and enjoy your Trance for a few minutes. For many of you, that is all it takes to experience Simultaneous Time. Now just as you did for your Star Origins, close your eyes for a few moments and sense your reincarnational existences. You may establish yourself within Simultaneous Time by thinking about what you enjoy about your life currently. On the theory that you enjoy certain pursuits now because you are enjoying them also in other lives, consider in these few moments, in which particular lives, within which particular timeframes you are also enjoying these pleasant pursuits. Use a light touch here. Here in SimeTime you are outside of the linear time construct. This is where you spend most of your "time." How are you spending your time in your other lives? When you feel as though you have received adequate effects, return to surface awareness.

Findings: Document your Findings as soon as possible after you come out of your Light Trance State.

Experiment: Identify Soul Family Members
This is a fun experiment that you may conduct often when you have a few minutes to explore.

Create a Light Trance State

Remembering what I have said about the Soul Family, relax within this altared state of Trance, and follow your breathing for a few moments. Consider that on the in-breath, you are receiving information about Soul Family Members that you are attempting to identify. Simply expect the information to come into your consciousness as you gently and methodically breathe in. As you breathe out, let go of that information. If you have an image of someone come to mind, let that image be released on the out-breath. If you have a strong feeling about someone on the in-breath, let that feeling be surrendered on the out-breath. Now you will have

SETH

perfect recall of all of this information when you come out of your Trance. Continue in this process of accessing the information as to whether it is valid or not valid. When you feel as though you have gathered enough material on possible Soul Family Members, gently return to surface awareness.

Findings: Document your Findings.

Chapter 3
Particulars of the Transition

"You are never more alive than the moment following your physical death."

The Other Side

The ultimate "surprise ending" for your life drama of existence, is that you are still conscious after your physical death. The body that you once inhabited lies before you. You have separated your consciousness from it, yet you still have a form. You have reclaimed your Etheric Body. You are once again reminded that you are never more alive than the moment following your physical death.

This is the truth of the matter, Dear Reader. Though many of you, I am sure, have been taught that you do not survive death, I am here to tell you that your personal consciousness does indeed survive the Transition. What you know and identify as your personality will carry on in other dimensions. In all of your lives, from all of the eras and time-frames that you have inhabited and will inhabit with your individual spark of Soul, you conclude each existence with a death of the physical body, yes that is true. But all of the familiar personalities that you gave life to in your times in the physical world, are there in your Home Dimension. They ARE you in the Home Dimension.

The Vitality of Consciousness

The Eternal Validity of the Soul, the sub-title for one of my books, describes perfectly what is recognized during this phase of the Transition. You realize that your consciousness is not destroyed at death. Indeed, the vitality of Evolutionary Consciousness is undeniable. It is an exhilarating and joyous recognition, this awareness of personal immortality. Now this is a major point of my book, and so I would like to digress a bit about it...

The awareness in the Afterlife that you are still conscious, still able to use your faculties, sweeps the books filled with religious protocols and religious dogmas from the shelves and sends them crashing to the floor. It upsets the paradigm so carefully tended by political and religious authorities. You realize that the indoctrination you have received from these authorities and others, was not for your benefit, or to secure a place in Heaven for you and your family, but meant purely to control

Death and the Afterlife

your thoughts, your imagery, your behaviors, your manifestation powers. That will be all for my soapbox moment.

Your Expectations are Realized

At the moment of death you will discover that your consciousness creates your reality after the Transition, just as surely as your consciousness creates your reality in the physical world. And just as you experience your physical reality through the filter of your beliefs and expectations, you will experience the Afterlife through the filter of your expectations and your beliefs about death. Each of you will experience at the time of your death, what you <u>expect</u> to experience, what you believe you <u>should</u> experience, what you were taught you <u>will</u> experience.

The Enactment

The reincarnational dramas and comedies of your preceding life continue during and after your Transition. Great care is taken by Soul to make certain that your recently transitioned consciousness is soothed and comforted. A Personalized Enactment is performed by members of your greater Soul Family for your benefit. They play roles of characters with whom you are familiar, that you expect to see after your death. The same was done for them at their Transition. You will participate in this dramatic presentation when you are called to do so after your death. This is done in an effort to once again introduce you to your Home Dimension existence. These enactments will continue until you are stabilized, until your consciousness becomes eager to see what is really going on. Now it may take years, centuries or merely a moment's time before you are prepared to see the truth of your condition. Let me say more about this intriguing phenomenon...

Personalized Afterlife Scenarios
The enactment will hold true until you can come to terms with the truth of your new reality. Here I do not wish to offend any of my readers. I assume that each of you has some religious conditioning that you bring to these discussions. Each of the religions tells a unique story about what to expect after physical death. And here is my point...

The human who has been raised as a Catholic, for example, and identifies themselves as a Catholic, who is steeped in that tradition, who believes the tenets of that practice, this person, at the end of their physical existence, because they create their reality as all of you do, will most likely witness a Catholic "crossing-over" to heaven, with all of the attributed symbols and emotional content.

Death and the Afterlife

Then, when these projections have served their purpose, by allowing the deceased to have a familiar experience without anxiety and fear, the images and emotions will fade away. Yet first, the expectations of the Ego/Intellect must play out on the screen of the Inner Senses.

Incidentally, this period of projecting your expectations of the death phenomenon and then reacting to this display as if it were happening <u>to</u> you, is quite similar to what you do as a <u>living</u> Reality Creator. You do feel as though your reality is happening <u>to</u> you, rather than the truth of the matter, which is that you are the work of art, yourself, and you are also the artist, creating you and your world. (See When You Walk Across the Room.)

The Onion Metaphor

Let me use the Onion Metaphor to describe to you how your Personalized Enactment unfolds in the Afterlife...

First, you create the mind that conceives of the God and the Goddess that you then create to worship. So in essence you worship yourself, or at least, your changing concept of self. In this case, the prayer energy that you invested in the creation of the God or Goddess that you worshiped in the physical world, is returned to you in the form of a personalized experience, in which you enjoy your anticipated interaction in the Afterlife with your God or Goddess of choice. Do you see? Your interactions would take place on one of the infinite layers of on-ion skin within the Home Dimension, and the Fifth and Sixth Dimensions. There is room for everyone here in this infinite domain of consciousness.

True Believers

Dear Reader, if you were taught by your parents and by your pastor that you were going to Hell when you died, because you had sinned, and you believed these suggestions, you would most probably have a hellish experience in The Transition. The length of this experience would be determined by the depth of your belief in Hell.

Of course, the opposite holds true for the saintly among you. You would most likely experience one of the Paradisiacal Dimensions. The experience would be fine-tuned to the criteria of your belief system.

The Facts of Death

What is revealed underneath these projections of the personal psyche, are the key enduring "facts of death," if you will pardon my play on words.

Death and the Afterlife

In all of the religious and mythological represen-
tations of what transpires at the time of physical
death and afterwards, there are some eternal truths.
These are the experiences of the transitioning Soul
that are common to all peoples:

- ❖ The consciousness realizes it is still functioning and still aware.

- ❖ The consciousness remembers its Star Origins and its connection to the Simultaneous
  Lives.

- ❖ The consciousness attempts to reorient itself
  to the new environment as the Ego/Intellect
  adapts.

- ❖ The consciousness begins to receive Guidance from the Higher Centers of Awareness.

- ❖ Once the Ego/Intellect has stabilized, the
  consciousness begins a review of the last life
  lived.

- ❖ Depending on the results of the review, the
  Soul will either return to Earth, or remain in
  the Home Dimension

This is a typical sequence of activity for the new-
ly transitioned Soul. Remember, however, that the
timing is different for each of you. Some will take
years, even lifetimes stabilizing the Ego/Intellect,
while others will take only a moment. Also remem-

SETH

ber, that some Souls immediately go back into physical existence after the Transition. For these Souls, the unfinished business they have left behind in the Third Dimension must be addressed immediately. And let me say this, <u>every Soul</u>, at some point, has made one of the immediate returns to physical life. This does not denote weakness or failure. In the Afterlife, as in physical life, the Soul seeks expression in terms of Value Fulfillment. If the Soul must make an immediate return to the Third Dimension, there is a very good reason for it. There may be very valuable Lessons to be learned by doing so.

Now let us examine what occurs within consciousness during the Transition experience. These are typical experiences of the transitioning Soul I am describing. Your personalized experience will be, of course, particular to you and your Soul Identity. But we may certainly comment on the experiences of most people to be used as a baseline for further understanding.

Holding On and Letting Go

Very simply, now... In your life in the Third Dimension, you create your Personal Reality Field through a dynamic process of Holding on and Letting Go. This I have covered in my last few books. For the average human, your existence is one of Holding

Death and the Afterlife

On, assessing, stabilizing, verifying, figuring things out, planning, and so on, and then Letting Go, allowing, surrendering, trusting, going with the flow. This dynamic follows you through the death process also. To the degree that you are Holding On, perhaps out of fear, your consciousness, your Soul, will remain in the physical body. Thus, you create a fear-filled Transition. To the degree that you Let Go and surrender to Love as you approach your Transition, you create Love within consciousness. You then experience a Loving death. You get what you focus on. You create your reality in all dimensions, through this Holding On and Letting Go dynamic. This is an important secret of the book. Remember this technique of surrendering to Love, and you will thrive in both the physical and the non-physical worlds.

Surrendering to Love
Through the surrendering process of Love, the Soul prepares itself to disengage from the physical body. Let me explain... Remember that in our theory, the Inner Senses are the senses of the Soul. The physical body has used the physical senses for the lifetime to orient to the physical plane and move about within the Personal Reality. Yet it is always the purview of the Inner Senses, to create with All That Is the physical world, that the human then experienc-

SETH

es with the physical senses. I have described realities as the outcomes or the results that ensue from the processing by the Inner Senses of the contents of the personal consciousness.

At death, it is no longer necessary for the physical senses to provide this feedback to the conscious mind. The physical senses begin to shut down. The Inner Senses become intensified within consciousness. The Soul, if I may say so, <u>comes forward</u>, and, using the creative energies of the Inner Senses, facilitates the creation of the Personalized Afterlife Scenario. This is the expectation of the Ego/Intellect of what will or what may occur at the time of death and afterwards that I have just described.

Difficult Transitions

If the Afterlife Scenario is of a negative type, one that includes bleedthroughs into the Nightmare or Hellish Dimensions, the negative realities will persist until the Transitioned consciousness surrenders in Love. And this is the avenue of escape, here. You Love and surrender in the perceived moment, and the next, and the next. Can you see the parallels between this suggested strategy for overcoming Negative Afterlife Realities, and those I suggest you use to transform the negative physical realities? This is the same principle of putting Love in action.

Death and the Afterlife

Physical Effects

Now what does the body feel during this surrendering process? I would say this: in the typical death experience for the modern human, you find yourself in a bed, let us say, in a reclining position. Your caregivers are attempting to keep you comfortable. The body is slowing down. The vital force is leaving the tissues. Symptoms of pain are felt, perhaps signaling to your caregivers that you require pain medication. The pain medications are administered and the body becomes sedated. At this point, the distractions of the physical body recede and the concerns of the Soul Identity come forward.

Now my students have asked me in the past about the value of medicating the dying person. They wonder whether the consciousness becomes confused. They wonder whether the administering of the medication interrupts or contaminates the dying process. My answer is, generally speaking, no it does not interrupt the dying process, and no it does not contaminate this process to sedate the dying person. Each person dies on their own terms, though this may not appear to be the case. Each person knows, at some level, when, where and how they will make the Transition.

SETH

Now the Ego/Intellect may become confused and defiant in the dying process. The Ego is used to running things and it will fight to maintain an appearance of control. Meanwhile the Intellect attempts to remember precedents for the experiences it is now witnessing. The Inner Senses of the Soul Identity, however, are always, even during the Transition, the true creators of what becomes experience or events, shall we say, in the physical and non-physical worlds. The Soul Identity is always clear, centered and totally aware of the circumstances, even though the physical body may be highly sedated. At this final stage of the Transition, the physical body construct becomes an impediment to the needs of the Soul Identity. Indeed, the Soul does vacate the body before physical death in some cases. It is all a matter of Lessons and Issues. However, as I have said, in most cases the Lesson is one of continuing the embodiment of Soul up until the moment of death.

The Ego/Intellect is Transformed
Normally your consciousness is transformed during the Transition. The personal consciousness we call the Ego/Intellect adapts itself automatically to the new environment. It remembers, via inputs from the Soul Identity, that this has happened before, in different bodies, in the Simultaneous Lives. In the

Death and the Afterlife

Post Transition Environment in which it finds it-self, this evolving identity construct quickly learns that Instant Manifestation is the norm. The Ego perspective of the Transitioning consciousness receives information from the Intellect, that is also adapting and changing to the new requirements, that negative emotion is not productive in the Afterlife. The Virtues of Humanity, Love, hope, faith, become the guides for creation in the new reality. You may see, I trust, how this may play out for the Ego/Intellect.

For example: A human who has perhaps used negative emotion, fear, treachery and so on to hurt others and control them in their previous life, would naturally use the same methods in the After-life. But within the Instant Manifestation environment of the Fourth Dimension, all is revealed. Your motives are there for all to see. (See also the Life Medallions.)

The Near Death Experience

The recounting of the Near Death Experience is a personalized account of what was experienced by the individual, but also, these accounts do often include observations of the basic sensory phenom-enon evident in all Transition scenarios. These elements I would call the Basics of The Transition.

SETH

These are the sensory aspects that underlie all of the personalized effects, emotions, images and so on that the transitioning figure projects onto the death process.

Now some of my students have asked me about the specific timing of these Basics of the Transition...

Outside of Time

There is no time, as you conceive of this idea, in the Transition and Post Transition Environments. Therefore, it becomes impossible to determine when precisely a Transition activity takes place. Many or all of the activities I describe here take place instantaneously. Because this occurs outside of time, and you are in your Etheric Body, your consciousness can hold all of this information and make sense of it. In the physical body, when you have a Near Death Experience, however, it is difficult to hold on to all of this data and remember it when you are revived. Yet it is often the case, as you know perhaps, that the key inspirational and educational elements of the NDE, are indeed remembered in vivid detail.

To those experiencing the NDE, these visionary events often act as wake-up calls. They are messages from your Higher Centers of Awareness that your Reality Creation strategies are deficient. Often what is suggested in these communications is that the experiencer have a major turnaround in thought, behavior and emotion. These messages are a form of Loving suggestions, you might say, from your progressed Self, warning you of the dangers that await you if you continue on your trajectory of development.

The Light

Your neuroscientists have theorized that the light that people experience while undergoing a Near Death Experience is best explained in terms of brain function. These scientists are coming from a "brain first" perspective, however. As you know, consciousness is the creator of all Reality Constructs, including the brain, including the world. Consciousness comes first.

My explanation for the light perceived in the NDE is this: The Light is the Love Light that creates realities. I have used the Love Light Matrix metaphor before in my books. When I describe to you that all realities, all dimensions are composed of Light, this is what I mean. The Love Light is my name for the light energy of All That Is. As the Consciousness Units merge together into infinite forms regulated by the Coordinate Points of electromagnetic energies, Light is formed. That is what the human sees with their Inner Senses when they have a Near Death Experience. And the human being undergoing a Transition into the Etheric Form has a similar experience.

The Exit of Soul

When does the Soul exit the physical body construct? This may occur long before the moment of death, but not usually. These types of strategies, whether to linger or to take an early exit, are up to the transitioning Ego/Intellect. Also sounding in on the discussion are the other players, here: the Soul Family throughout time, The Council, the Spiritual Hierarchy. It is a collaborative effort to determine if the Soul will exit sooner rather than later, or after being forced out, in a sense, by a body that is exhausted of life force. There is no right or wrong way to extract the Soul from the physical body. In fact, often, humans will exit in a preferred fashion, showing a certain flair of personality that they demonstrated while in the life. The impatient personality in life, becomes impatient to exit the body, and does so, as soon as possible.

These decisions are part of the Soul Contract you make before you enter into the body before you are born. However, as usual, the Contract may be changed and amended at any point in the existence through a free-will choice to do things differently. You may alter the Contract up until the time of the Transition.

In the next two experiments, please hold a Good Humor thought as you proceed. These exercises should be approached without negative emotion.

End of Chapter Experiments

Experiment: Your Imagined Death

This is an Experiment we first covered in our book Soul Mate Soul Family. It entails a visualization of what you might experience on your deathbed, directly before the Transition to the Home Dimension. Your visualization will, of course, be different than others might create. The idea is to visualize the death scene to see what Lessons may have been avoided that are now in plain view with the imminent death experience upon you. Please consider, then, this death scene as occurring in your very current reality: at the age you are now, in the home in which you now live, with the people around you who are in your life currently.

SETH

Create a Light Trance State

Now simply relax, as usual, as you rest comfortably in a quiet room where you can remain undisturbed for 15 minutes. Breathe deeply. Close your eyes and imagine that you are on a beach somewhere or in another location that you have visited where you experienced complete calm and relaxation.

This is your imagination at work here and you have complete control over the activities in this experiment. You are, in fact, observing your self from a vantage point near the ceiling of the room you are in. Imagine the particulars of your deathbed scene.

Feel the comfort of the sheets and blankets around you. Look at the room and notice the color of the walls, any pictures on the walls, any details you would care to notice about the room.

Now you allow memories to come to your consciousness, memories of painful events from your past. These memories you forgive and heal in the moment of remembering: Courageously, you see. Reenactments of experiences from your past when you were abused, neglected, unloved, or you were abusive to others may arise. In the moment of

Death and the Afterlife

memory, forgive yourself and others immediately and then let that material fade away.

Courageous Forgiveness is your motto here as you imagine yourself surrounded by the people who have hurt you and those you have hurt in your life. One by one you look them in the eye, and with your boundless compassion you forgive them and your-self simultaneously. It's exhilarating to be free of all that dead weight. You may feel like laughing out loud you are so completely cleansed of the trauma of the past. When you feel it is time to come out of Trance, slowly come up to surface awareness.

Findings: Document your Findings immediately.

Experiment: Personalized Transition Scenario
Keep your eyes open for this experiment.

Create a Light Trance State

Write down on a piece of paper what you feel might be your Personalized Transition Scenario that you will experience at the end of your life. This would include what your parents have told you, what reli-gious leaders have told you, what family and friends or any person or any institution has told you about what happens after physical death. This account-ing will describe what you believe will occur. Your beliefs have thought, image and emotion behind them. If the accounting is lacking in the desired positive emotions, then amend that description to create a more empowered and Loving experience. Read the amended accounting to yourself and internalize the new script over time. I think you may see where I am going with this.

Findings: Document your Findings.

Chapter 4
The Afterlife

"In the beginning, you will experience what you expect to experience."

The Paradisiacal Dimensions

Does Heaven exist? This is a common question presented to me in workshops and in phone sessions. My stock answer is this: It exists if you believe it exists. Let me make my point...

The theorized Paradisiacal Dimensions would be those Gestalts of Consciousness founded on and energized by the Virtues of Humanity, as we call them: Love, Courage, compassion, and so on. Now my question to you is this. How much evidence for the existence of Heaven do you see in your Personal Reality? If Heaven is the energetic repository of all of the good deeds, Loving thoughts, selfless acts of Courage, and other positive emotion contents of humanity at the time, tell me if heaven exists, at least in the idealized state I believe you are referencing. It does exist if you think it exists.

SETH

The Loving Person

The Loving, Courageous, compassionate person creates a Paradise that they enjoy in the Afterlife. Throughout the physical existence, suppose that this person has focused primarily on the positive. They have given generously to others. They have shown compassion when appropriate. They are expert at doing good deeds for others. They are known as an enlightened Soul. They are awakened, let us say, to the truth of the Loving Universe. Their very natural expectation, is that, after the physical existence, they will enter into an ideal state of Afterlife. Their expectation is realized after the Transition, for they, like everyone else, will at first experience what they believe they will experience.

The Afterlife Experience is always personalized, however, according to the specific criteria of the beliefs. For this reason, each human's experience of the Afterlife Paradise will be different from all others. A different Heaven for all of you, you see. This is my humor, Dear Reader. Though naturally, each account will vary from others according to cultural and personal biases, for these projections are always based on what was experienced and believed in the preceding existence.

Death and the Afterlife

The Hellish Dimensions

The Hellish Dimensions also exist in infinite variety. Every nuance of negative emotion has been explored by consciousness within the human experience and is registered in detail in these dimensions. These are the etheric locales, the Gestalts of Consciousness, that inspire visitors from the Tibetan Buddhist, the Christian and the innumerable other religious paths, to conceive of the <u>opposites</u> of Paradise. These are the dimensions fueled on fear, anger, neglect, despair and helplessness, that act as a counterpoint to the stories of Heaven and the idealized Afterlife destinations.

The Hellish Dimensions, too, have their place in the Afterlife. In a sense, you might say that the demons and other denizens of the Hellish Dimensions have earned their place. These Gestalts of Consciousness have been supported throughout the millennia by the negative emotional energy of humanity. Every hateful thought, each act of revenge and violence, every negative image entertained within the mental environment of the human collective, gives birth to and helps to sustain these Hellish Dimensions.

SETH

Is the Christian Hell a "real" place? Yes, it is. You might say that the so-called "sinner" on Earth, who believes in their religion and who "buys-into" the concept of sin and punishment, effectively supports the Hellish Dimensions with that fear energy. The self-described sinner who believes they are evil, for example, contributes to the creation of evil environments or dimensions. When they make their Transition, they may very well take their place in the Hellish Dimensions, in order to "pay their dues." Of course these negative environments are based on some very dramatic mis-perceptions.

The Etheric Body

Now I have suggested that the Etheric Body is your vehicle in the Afterlife and in your Dreaming Time, just as your physical body is your vehicle in the Third Dimension. However, whereas you move through your innumerable lives in the reincarnational cycle, inhabiting physical bodies of various types, your Etheric Body remains constant and unchanging throughout. You might think of this Light Body as representing the culmination of all of your experiences as a Soul. It would be unchanging, eternal, constant, you see.

Death and the Afterlife

Your Etheric Body has a number of interesting and valuable features that serve you-the-Soul when you are in your Home Dimension. When you are in your Etheric Body, it is an easy matter to travel instantly to any desired location, in the physical or the non-physical worlds. You simply focus your Intent on that location and you are there. In the Afterlife of the Unknown Reality, you are completely comfortable and knowledgeable. You have spent your Afterlife in the non-physical world within this Etheric Body, and "you know the territory," so to speak, quite well.

The Energy Medallions

Your Etheric Body is composed of Love Light energy, vibrating at the signature frequency that identifies you to others in the Afterlife reality. (You may view the front cover of our book *The Next Chapter in the Evolution of the Soul* to see an artist's rendition of my Etheric Body.)

In the Home Dimension you wear around your necks a type of energy medallion that exhibits to others the particulars of your lives lived. It is a summary, in fact, of Lessons, experiences and future plans for Reality Creation. It is within this medallion or vortex of information that all of you "read" about your fellows. You use your Inner Senses to pick up on the communication streams from these medallions telepathically. Now in the physical dimension we refer to this display as the Auric Field, the Emotional Body, and so on. We are talking about the same phenomenon: the exposition of important ideas, imagery, and emotion relative to lives lived and to be lived.

Multidimensional Experiencing

Your existence in the Afterlife is one of a perception of the Fourth, Fifth and Sixth Dimensions. You are also capable of visiting and viewing the other systems I speak of in my books, including the Probable Realities. Just as you would take a vacation to visit foreign lands while in the physical body on earth, in the Etheric Body you are able to travel, in a fraction of a second, to the other systems of reality. A dimension of Love exists, as I have said, where the creation of negative emotion is not permitted. Civilizations that exist on other planets in your solar system and elsewhere are also easily accessible. By thinking about it you are there in a moment.

As a Soul, having lived countless lives, and having experienced the Transition at the end of those lives, you have naturally been drawn to particular systems of reality expression that suit you, that you enjoy. In some of these systems, just as you do on

Death and the Afterlife

Earth, you make friends with other Souls and visit them in your Etheric Body. In the Afterlife you visit them also.

Star Life

Now I opened up this discussion with my suggestions to you that your origins are in several different Star Systems. This is true. However, I will now enlarge that description somewhat, by reminding you that both in your physical existences and in your etheric afterlives, you are quite capable of returning to your Star Origins, and sensing the generative power of that existence. Also remember, I am describing to you my Essential Metaphors here. Your Star Life existence, then, is a metaphor for All That Is as this Primary Creative Gestalt first created human consciousness within an etheric form.

Visitations to Reincarnational Lives

In the Afterlife, it is a common practice for you to visit Soul Family members in the multiple timeframes in which you experienced lives together. You are not limited to observing your most recent life experience. Often the transitioned Soul yearns for a reunion type of experience, and may visit many different lives to see what has changed since they were embodied in the life they have just exited. These visits from the Afterlife account for the experiences some people have of "feeling the presence" of a departed friend or family member. I would say that these people are using their Inner Senses to experience a very real phenomenon.

The Two Mirrors

The onion comparison served us in our description of the holographic dimensions of All That Is. Now in terms of the Star Life Existence, your Simultaneous Lives and other existences, consider the illusion created when you stand in between two facing mirrors. You see in the mirror in front of you the reflection from the mirror behind you of seemingly multiple yous. Consider here that each of those reflections of you represents a Simultaneous life, or an existence in the Spiritual Hierarchy, or an existence in your Home Dimension, or one in a Probable Reality that has not been manifested, or an existence in The Council, or a life within a system so alien to you that you cannot describe it. This comparison works very well for us, here, for the illusion is very striking and does indeed evoke the sense of multidimensional experiencing perceived by you through your Higher Centers of Awareness.

The Library

There exists in extra-dimensional reality a Gestalt of Consciousness that is infinitely vast and compre-

Death and the Afterlife

hensive. This Energy Body is an etheric repository for the Ancient Wisdom, primarily, but it also holds the whole of humanity's experiences, past, present and future, in a concentrated form, you might say. This is possible via the properties of my theorized Consciousness Units. The counterpart to this in other systems would be the Akashic Records or the Collective Unconscious. In my Teaching we call it The Library, to keep it simple for an easy understanding of this fundamental concept.

When you tune-in to this Gestalt of Consciousness while still in the physical body, it is possible to find answers to whatever questions you might have on any subject. You might think of The Library as consisting of an infinite number of data banks, holding all of the knowledge and experiencing of humanity. You ask and you receive the answers to your questions, as though you were operating a very powerful super computer.

When you are in the Afterlife, the Library is available to you also. Indeed, after you have made your Transition, you may find that it will prove to be your favorite destination. The resources within the Gestalt of Consciousness assist you in your research into your various lives.

SETH

Remember, this is an Essential Metaphor for a phenomenon that is indescribable. It is beyond words. However, let me say this... The Feeling-Tone you sense when you are in The Library and receiving answers to your questions is one of Instant Awakening. The secrets of the universe are revealed to you and you are elevated, grateful and inspired.

End of Chapter Experiments

Experiment: Sense Your Etheric Body

Your physical body in the Third Dimension is composed of the same Consciousness Units that make up your Etheric Body in the Home Dimension. In this Experiment, you may get a sense of the truth of this statement.

Now you are always in your Etheric Body, however you are only aware of it when you are in the dream state, or possibly when you are in Trance or in meditation. There is a distinctive Feeling-Tone that you associate with being in your Etheric Body.

Create a Light Trance State

Relax and focus on your breath. As you breathe in, allow your breath to fill your lungs and stomach, and as you do, visualize the healing properties of breath going to those parts of your body that need

Death and the Afterlife

to be balanced, invigorated and healed. As you breathe out, imagine all of the anxiety, fear and pain you may be experiencing to flow out of your body and be neutralized. Breathing in and breathing out. You are reaching the precise frequency of thought and emotion that you require to experience your Etheric Body. You know this. You have done this through your innumerable lives. Still focusing on the breath, imagine that on the next inhale, you will flash-in to a momentary awareness of your Etheric Body. It's easy to do this, as you are only tuning in for an in-breath. When you receive an effect, a momentary Feeling-Tone of ecstasy and lightness, acknowledge it and focus on the out- breath as you again return to an acknowledgment of your physical body. Over time you will be able to lengthen the time of experiencing the Etheric Body to include both the in-breaths and the out-breaths. You will learn how to regulate your awareness in this way.

When you have received some effects, slowly return to surface awareness.

Findings: Document your Findings as to the Feeling-Tones you experienced during the Experiment.

Experiment: Visit the Library

In this Experiment you will visit The Library. You

will have total recall of what you experienced there, so that you may document it at the end of the Experiment.

This Experiment, like all of the others in this book, is an exercise in co-creation. You will use your Intent to visit this etheric locale, and then you will fill in the details with your own consciousness. You are collaborating with your Higher Centers of Awareness when you do this.

Create a Light Trance State

Relax and breathe deeply as you enter your Trance State. Your goal here is to put a familiar face upon this etheric concept of the Library. Now it is easy for you to remember libraries from your past that you visited as a child or as an adult. There is a distinct Feeling-Tone you get when you are in a library. There is visual, tactile, auditory and olfactory information available to you. Using your Intent, direct your consciousness to visit the Library, as you are guided by your Inner Senses. Perhaps you can see the architecture of the building with its pillars, granite and marble. Perhaps you can hear the echoes of your footsteps as you walk into the Library itself. Perhaps you can feel texture of the pages as you turn them. Perhaps you can smell the

Death and the Afterlife

musty air in the room that holds the documentation of EVERYTHING.

Now if you feel comfortable doing so, ask a question you wish answered. The answer may come to you visually, as in a book opening to a specific page with writing on it. Or it may come aurally, as in hearing the answer spoken to you, and so on.

When you feel you have received some effects, promise yourself that you will return to the Library soon and slowly return to surface awareness,

Findings: Immediately document your Findings from your visit to the Library.

Chapter 5
Holographic Life Review

"The Display allows for instantaneous reliving of key elements and experiences of the life."

The Life of Learning

Your lives are opportunities to identify your Issues and learn your Lessons. As Mark very often reminds me, this learning may take place in joyful appreciation. And this is true. Yet none of you are perfect, and so "mistakes are made," as they say. The mistakes come from the quite natural and common mis-perceptions of the Ego/Intellect identity. The Ego believes it is in charge, as you know. It will defend its territory - your consciousness, your Personal Reality Field - by giving you false and misleading information. For the Ego prefers the way things are, rather than the improved reality you may have in mind.

On the other hand, the Soul counsels you to surrender to Love in the moment. But how often do you obey the suggestions of the Soul? The mistakes

SETH

of the Ego/Intellect, then, often bring you into conflict with other humans through the creation of negative emotions. Rather than listen to your heart, your Soul, your Higher Self, you listen to the Ego/Intellect and this results in conflict, hurt feelings, errors in judgment, and the other elements that create a troubled relationship with others and with the Self.

The Life Review

Yes, your lives are lives of learning, as though you are in a school. Using that same comparison, your Afterlife may be thought of as a type of higher education. After your Transition, your graduation, you move into a different curriculum of learning, one in which what was learned on Earth is used to create a type of dissertation or master work. I am pushing this comparison to its limits, here... In a type of research study, you pursue an investigation of your life in its entirety.

You are in multi-dimensional reality, outside of time in the Home Dimension. You are able to experience the physical life you have lived previously, while you are still in this other dimension. This is possible through the creative interface that we may call the Holographic Display.

Death and the Afterlife

The Holographic Display

This is an etheric display that you create through the use of your Inner Senses. It takes the form of whatever you may be familiar with in the previous life, that would constitute a playback of scenes from your existence. Thus, a tribal member from a collective centuries ago, having made their Transition, would possibly visualize the display in terms of a type of vivid dream or waking vision that they experienced while in the physical body. This is what they knew. The display is self-created from what is known, you see.

A modern transitioner would possibly create a display that had the features of a movie screen or perhaps a television or computer display. Yet ALL creations of this etheric viewing experience have the same features that make it a very powerful "instrument" indeed.

The Holographic Display allows for instantaneous reliving of key elements and experiences of the life, or even a complete and thorough review of the life, in a fraction of a second. This is possible for you are no longer subject to the dictates of time and space while you perceive within your Home Dimension. Being outside of time places you in this non-linear environment of consciousness.

SETH

Cause-and-effect are not IN effect in this context. This is difficult material to describe, yet I will press onward...

The Holographic Display allows you to experience your current existence in your Home Dimension AND your complete existence you have just left, simultaneously. It is holographic, in other words. You are in it. You ARE the Holographic Display instrument. Do you see? In the Etheric Body you utilize your Inner Senses exemplified in this Holographic Display perspective. Because you are in it and you are it, it makes little sense to speak in terms of "returning" to the Past Life and examining various aspects of it, and then "returning" to your Home Dimension, for everything happens simultaneously and instantaneously, for your are in it, and you are it. I have placed some informative subtext in this description that will guide you to a deeper understanding of this concept, if you allow it.

Making Desired Corrections

The object of this process of the Life Review is to consider when and where within the previous life, you have made perceived mistakes in your Reality Creation. Often these mistakes involve the perception of hurting another human. Another common perceived error is NOT doing something that was

Death and the Afterlife

very much desired at the time; the road not taken, you see. Regrets for what might have been often drive these Afterlife assessments.

Now you are deeply connected to Soul here in the Afterlife. Your view, therefore, is through the lenses of Loving Understanding and Courage, primarily. The focus becomes one of determining where Love was absent, perhaps, and where Love was needed. The focus is on where you failed to act out of fear. You did not do something greatly desired for you were not Courageous.

The dynamics of this holographic interaction between your Afterlife Identity and your Past Life appear to be complex on the surface, however, they are very elementary in fact. You simply begin to tune-in on those events from the Past Life that need to be remedied. Perhaps you carried the burden of guilt and resentment for many years. These negative events are burned into your memory. They exist in the past, this is true. However, through this etheric technology of The Display, you may replay those sequences of the existence, and re-experience them in detail with your Inner Senses. You are eager. You are motivated in this Afterlife to make amends. This is what the Soul suggests: that you "make things right." It is a necessary activity for you to <u>consider</u> before you may continue. By this, I mean, you are not forced to make amends. You consult with your Guides and decide to correct the errors and you do or you may defer these unlearned Lessons to other lives.

Your Guides Assist You

Your Higher Centers of Awareness, your Guides, represent YOU at a progressed stage in your development. When you ask for help from your Guides while in the physical vehicle, then, you are asking your progressed Self and your fully integrated consciousness from the future, for advice. This same dynamic exists in the Afterlife. For this reason, you could truthfully say that you are taking your own advice when you receive counseling on what to do about correcting your perceived mistakes in the previous life. Now a full explanation of how you contact yourself from the future in these relationships with your Guides, would fill another volume. For now please attempt to see the big picture here in this explanation. It may help to view our illustration **A Map of the Afterlife** on the following page.

MAP OF THE AFTERLIFE

SPIRITUAL HIERARCHY

THE COUNCIL

SIXTH DIMENSION

FIFTH DIMENSION

GUIDES

INSTANT MANIFESTATION

HOME DIMENSION

THE AFTERLIFE

THIRD DIMENSION

EARTH

LINEAR TIME

NONLINEAR TIME

NONLINEAR TIME

SETH

Third Dimensional Effects

Your Soul Family members in the Third Dimension know when you are around and when you are attempting to make corrections in the Holographic Display of your life. They may entertain a fond memory of you in these moments. They may grieve for you at these times. There may be certain symbols and signs that are apparent when they come to visit. These signs are presented to your awareness so that you will know when they are around, and you may have communications with them.

Of course you may perceive through the Holographic Display perspective while you are still in the physical body. This is what you do in the dream state and in the Trance State when you are engaged in the Experiments I offer in my new books. Yet, when you are in your Home Dimension, without the physical body and its encumbrances, the Inner Senses are easily initialized and used with fluency immediately. While you are still in the body, it does take some practice to learn how to function in the Etheric Body. You are obliged to learn the skills and practices common to the new environment.

Momentary Home Dimension Bleedthroughs

"My entire life played out before me." You-the-reader have possibly experienced the phenomenon of having your "entire life flash before your eyes." This is similar to but is to be distinguished from the Holographic Life Review. I would call these brief reviews "momentary bleedthroughs" into the Home Dimension that you experience while still in the physical body. Conditions are met by your consciousness that allow for these small bleedthroughs. They are not accidental, by any means, nor or they pre-destined. These Spontaneous Life Reviews come at appropriate times. They are teaching aids of your greater self, your Higher Centers of Awareness.

Notice how they often present your Issues and Lessons in a type of educational format. There is no mistaking the message here in these reviews. You are being called to look at how you are creating your reality currently. You are often advised by the Feeling-Tones in these bleedthroughs, to improve your Reality Creation for your own betterment and for the good of others. These are the same concerns considered in the Holographic Life Review.

End of Chapter Experiments

Experiment: The Holographic Display
All of you have dreamed, therefore, all of you have experienced the Holographic Display. If you have experimented with your Dream Time, and created

a perspective of Lucid Dreaming, this is also an example of the phenomenon. With that in mind...

Create a Light Trance State

Now we will bring you a bit deeper into the Trance for this Experiment. You may tune-in to that pleasant state of consciousness that directly leads to dreaming. I have spoken of this state of awareness before in my books. It is that moment in which you surrender to the pull of the Dream Time. The sleep hormones are creating ecstasy within your mental environment. Gently you assure your Ego/Intellect that all is well, you shall return after your journey. Then you let go. You go with the flow of consciousness. You put on your Etheric Body and leave your physical body safely where you are.

Thinking in terms of a Life Review, use your Intent to focus your Holographic Display apparatus on your birth, or on your early childhood. If this is too uncomfortable for you, tune-in to the time from your past when you felt the most happiness. Now, simply allow this Holographic Display to process the life from then until now, and feed it back to you in terms of sensory stimuli. You may envision the display as a movie screen at the theater, perhaps. You are the only one seated in the theater. It

Death and the Afterlife

is a private showing. You are also the operator of the Display, and so you turn the dial or press the button to initiate the playback of your life upon the screen. When you feel you have received sufficient data from this Experiment, slowly come up to surface awareness.

Findings: Document your Findings.

Chapter 6
The Council et al

"The idea of a single spiritual authority, a supreme being, dominates the world religions."

Non-physical Beings

All of the non-physical beings that were the focus of your physical existence are with you in the Afterlife. This includes, potentially of course, the God and the Goddess, and all of the spiritual beings celebrated in all of the spiritual practices of Earth. By focusing on them during your life, you bring them life. They assisted you in physical life, even though you may not have been aware of it, and in the Afterlife they assist you as well. Indeed, the communications between you and your non-physical Guides become much clearer and stronger in the Afterlife.

Your Guides

You often meet your Guides in childhood. If you were fortunate enough to have a caregiver who read fairy tales to you as a child, the probabilities are quite good that you were able to create an imaginal context for experiencing these non-physical beings in adulthood. This is how it works in every culture. What you may call the "acceptable and validated" non-physical beings of a particular collective, are given life through the tradition of storytelling. The mind of a child is fertile soil in which to plant these seeds. If those initial storytelling efforts were consistent and positive, the odds are good that you are still, as an adult now, maintaining those connections, those etheric friendships with the non-physical beings.

And as I have said before in my lectures and in my books, the caregiver that allows the child to develop relationships with the so-called "imaginary playmate," and allows for the relationship to continue into adolescence and adulthood, is doing the child a great favor. The etheric playmate often matures into the Energy Personality, the Guide, the Genie, even as the child matures into an imaginative, creative, empowered adult.

The God of You

After your Transition, these childhood Guides "meet you at the station," in a manner of speaking. They are with you when you come into physical form. They are with you throughout your lifetime. They assist you as you make your Transition. They are there to greet you in your Home Dimension. Who are they? At the risk of repeating myself, they represent YOU at a future stage of evolution. Indeed, ALL of the non-physical beings that you associate with consciously or unconsciously, ARE you. Your progressed consciousness, the God of you, looks back at you and Loves you from the future. This aspect of you seems like a God or a Goddess, for it does have that charisma and power that is associated with the Divine. Nonetheless, it is you. Remember, when I suggested that an amnesia comes over you, as you are re-born within the human collective in one of your Simultaneous Existences? In the amnesia you forget your power. You forget that you create realities. You forget that you are a God, a Goddess. But after the Transition, your true state becomes quite clear again. With this realization, the fear and anxiety melt away. It is replaced by Courageous Loving Understanding as you once again take your place in the Pantheon of Divine beings, known collectively as the human race.

The Spiritual Hierarchy

The Spiritual Hierarchy are those Etheric Beings who have experienced lifetimes on Earth over the millennia. They have learned all that here is to know about the Third, Fourth, Fifth and Sixth Dimensions. They are highly evolved Beings of Light who act in service to other evolving Souls. They are

SETH

Guides, essentially, that you will consult with in matters of your plans for further incarnations.

I have received some criticism for referring to this Gestalt of Consciousness as a hierarchy. My critics are correct, in that, there is no such thing as a being higher than another being. However, I use the time and space distinctions and conventions common to spiritual discussions in your world. There is no before and after. There is not time and space. There is no up and down. There is no such thing as a Supreme Being. All beings are supreme in truth. All beings are equal, for all beings are composed of All That Is. Yet, in order for you-the-reader to make sense of this esoteric material, I feel I must use terms with which you are familiar. If you cannot tolerate this concept of a Spiritual Hierarchy, please think of it in terms of spiritual evolution. These beings are simply more evolved than the average Soul, for they have experienced more. That is all. The more experienced Soul is thought to have more wisdom, and thus, would tend to provide more truthful and useful guidance than a younger, less-evolved Soul.

Also please note, that, just as your Guides represent you at a more evolved station in Soul Evolution, the members of the Spiritual Hierarchy and of The Council ARE you, at the culmination of your Soul's evolution. These Energy Beings may successfully guide you, for they <u>are</u> you. They are pulling you, in a manner of speaking, towards them so that you may take your place within them. If this is too etheric for you to consider... These beings represent your best potential, what we call the Best Case Scenario in my books. They are the ideal result one may expect to come from the manifestation activities of your Soul in the human and etheric forms.

The Council

The Council is composed of members of the Spiritual Hierarchy. I define them as highly evolved beings that advise Souls on incarnations for their spiritual evolution. These Gestalts of Consciousness act as your personal Guides, your representatives, you might say, in the Afterlife. Whereas the Spiritual Hierarchy is composed of an infinite number of personalized Energy Gestalts, The Council represents those few Guides that have been in your service over the course of all of your existences.

Bargaining With the Council et al

Some of you have met the members of The Council. If you have had a brush with death, either through an accident or other means, you have probably met The Council. If you are visually oriented, you may

SETH

have seen them as robed figures standing over you or in the clouds, as Mark has done. If you favor the auditory sensations, perhaps you heard voices counseling you, assuring you, warning you.

Now The Council is another of my Essential Metaphors. The actual phenomenon of this interaction between your Higher Centers of Awareness and these representatives from All That Is, is difficult to put into words. If I were to attempt to describe this communication, the results might be similar to our little inspirational essays we presented in our book *All That Is*.

I believe that this visual, of the robed figures in the sky, or suspended in front of you, that many of you reference in connection with the Ancestors, the Intergalactic Beings, and others, conveys the essence of the phenomenon quite well. However, I would make a few changes in the interests of accuracy.

- ❖ The members of the Council are neither male nor are they female. They represent the human energies, the human Spirit undifferentiated. The perceiver projects gender onto these Beings of Light.

- ❖ They are not elderly, necessarily.

- ❖ They do not dress in robes, necessarily, but are

84

attired in the individual projections of those witnessing them. You view them through the lenses of your beliefs and your history.

Talking to Your Progressed Self

Now the bargaining that takes place between the transitioning Soul and the members of The Council is centered on the old question of whether Issues and Lessons were addressed appropriately and learned in the life. As I said, there is no judgment, no guilt, no embarrassment around the subject matter. The Soul Identity is beyond these types of negative self-assessing. The Soul Identity, which also represents the evolved and adapted Ego/Intellect of the Transitioning human, observes the replay of the life through the Holographic Display, (See Chapter 5) and consults with The Council on whether the terms in the Soul Contract were fulfilled.

The Subject for Discussion

In a very general sense, the goal of Soul Evolution is to experience ALL that may be experienced in human and etheric form. The process is one of transforming the negative into the positive with Love, Loving Understanding and Courage. The Virtues of Humanity are thus realized in this transformation process. Generally speaking, where the human deviated from expressing the Virtues of Humanity,

SETH

and instead re-created the negative emotions, and participated in negative behaviors and creating negative realities for themselves and others, you could say that the they failed to keep the terms of the Soul Contract.

These deficits will play a part in creating a new Soul Contract, should the Soul wish to move forward with a new life, and a new opportunity to express the Virtues of Humanity in a human body.

I realize, this is beginning to sound like the negotiations that purportedly take place at the gates of Heaven with St. Peter and the other metaphysical beings. The negotiation metaphor is common in the accounts of the Transition phenomenon one reads in the sacred texts of the cultures of the world.

The Supreme Being

The idea of a single spiritual authority, a supreme being, dominates the world religions. Thus, this idea dominates and overshadows the Transition activities of much of humanity. A large percentage of humans exiting your system, have been schooled in one or more of the world religions, and the symbols, characters, and stories from these scriptures are effectively imprinted on the identities of these people. For this reason, the Afterlife is replete with

Death and the Afterlife

the enactments of Transition and Afterlife scenarios suggested in the scriptures from these religions.

As you know, the non-physical beings of all types are empowered and endure through the prayer energy focused upon them by human beings. This energy, projected onto the Supreme Being of choice, helps to sustain these Gestalts of Consciousness within the extra-dimensional planes in which they exist. If you have focused on a Supreme Being in your spiritual practices in the Third Dimension, you will likely experience the return of your energy investment in that Gestalt of Consciousness, by participating in Afterlife dramas documented in the sacred texts of your religion.

The Mythological Domain

Currently your popular culture is enjoying a renaissance of interest in the mythological domain of collective consciousness. Millions of you enjoy vicariously the adventurous pursuits of vampires, dragons, angels, fairies, elementals, super heroes and other characters. As you participate in these media events, you seed alternate realities within the collective consciousness with your reality creation energies. This is how the mythological domain is given life, you see, through your fervent thought and emotion energy. In the Afterlife, you

will experience a return of your emotional investment in these media of mythological drama. This
is no different than what the Catholic or the Meth-
odist or the Buddhist experiences in the post-Tran-
sition world. All of you receive in the etheric world
what you focused on in the physical world. The saga
continues. The story unfolds.

End of Chapter Experiments

Experiment: Meeting your Guides

In this experiment you may be revisiting an event
from your past when you were in touch with these
non-physical beings. However, if you have yet to
meet your Guides, simply follow the instructions
with an expectation that you will be successful. Now
you will be able to remember all of this when you
come out of Trance. That is my suggestion to you.

Create a Light Trance State

Relax and close your eyes, if you have not already
done so. Follow your breath and allow each exhale
to bring you closer to the etheric domain of your
Guides. You know how it feels when you are in touch
with your Guidance. Generate that Feeling-Tone
now within your consciousness. Use your breath
to navigate the etheric world and find your Guides.
Each inhale gives you direction. Each exhale pulls

Death and the Afterlife

you closer to your destination. Your Guides exist in the Fourth Dimension and beyond. Visualize your Etheric Form traveling through the dimensions.

When you have reached the domain of your Guides, look around and see who is there. Do you see familiar faces? Who is there to greet you? If you see faces that are not familiar, ask for their names. Ask if your Guides have anything to tell you. When you have received some information on your Guides, slowly return to surface awareness.

Findings: Document your experiences in meeting your Guides.

Chapter 7
Returning

"You have a tendency to choose those roles that will help you experience your Issues and learn your Lessons."

The Decision to Return

For those of you who will take on another body in the Third Dimension of Earth, there is a great deal to consider. To return, and in what body, and in what location, and for what purpose, is a group decision to be made by your adapting Ego/Intellect, your Soul Family members past, present and future and your Guides and other advisors. Yet your Soul Identity makes the final decision, for it will be you who will undergo the future incarnation. Let me say a few words about this...

In the Home Dimension, the participants are not subject to the constraints of time and space that those of you in the Third Dimension must respect. It becomes possible for all concerned to conceive of the complex strategy and logistics necessary to support the new voyage of Soul into the physical domain. The participants who will have an influence within the life of the future incarnated Soul, will each have a broad agenda established that will guide their behaviors in the Soul Family collective. You might think of this broad agenda as a type of script that the Soul Family member will use as a simple reference point. Going along with this metaphor of a performance, then, for free-will is the rule within human consciousness in the Third Dimension, the suggestions in the script are entirely optional, and the Soul Family member may use the telepathic suggestions received from this script to improvise their role within Soul Family interactions.

Then it is within this improvisational format of the reincarnational lives that all Soul Family members commit to a Soul Contract agreement, defining, in broad terms again, their role in the performance.

For example: A particular Soul Family member may agree to play a very cursory role in the life of the returning Soul. The Soul Contract would stipulate that within the Telepathic Network. But because the terms of the Contract are so broad, the Soul Family Member may decide to play a much more important and decisive role. As this occurs during the existence, according to the free-will choices of the participants, the Soul Contract is revised to reflect the new role, and these changes are broadcast throughout the Telepathic Network.

Timely Choices

Now the returning Soul may enter into a new life at any point in time. In other words, they may incarnate into a past timeframe, into a future timeframe, or return to the timeframe from which they came. Normally, the returning Soul will enter into the consciousness of a baby and begin the reincarnational journey from the beginning of that life, from the birth.

Though it is rare, the returning Soul may enter into the consciousness of a mature child or adult. This is usually not thought of as invasive by the host consciousness. It is not thought of as possession. It is usually experienced as an expansion of consciousness.

Reincarnational Endpoint

Of course, the decision may be made to not incur further lives in the Third Dimension. This relates to the Old Soul concept we speak about in my books. The Old Soul has encountered many lives and explored all avenues of Reality Creation for its own

SETH

educational purposes, and for All That Is. There comes a time when the need to engage the physical dimension of Earth becomes less urgent. The Soul has learned as much as it needs to learn. The decision may then be made to no longer incarnate on Earth. The Soul, in a sense, "retires" to an existence that does not include Earth life.

I have told my students over the years, that, when they have reached the limits of what is required for them to experience in the physical body, they too, just as I have, may retire to an Afterlife of study, perhaps, or one of inter-dimensional travel, or one of teaching, or one of assisting others in the dream state.

Afterlife Roles

For those of you who choose to stay in the Afterlife, and not return to the physical world, there are many choices of roles that you may adopt, depending on what is of interest to you. You favor adopting particular roles in the Afterlife, just as you favor adopting particular roles in the physical world. There is a difference, however. When you go into the physical world in a new body, and proceed upon a new life of Learning, you have a tendency to choose those roles that will help you to experience your Issues and learn your Lessons. That is the point of the Soul

Death and the Afterlife

Contract and that is why you return to physical life time and time again.

Your lives on Earth are primarily concerned with how you will react to the negative emotions that you experience. The Earth Plane is a proving ground, as I have said before, for the negative emotions and for the reincarnational dramas that grow from the negative emotions. Thus you see an average human taking on the role of martyr, persecutor, saboteur, victim, masochist, and so on, all in the name of experiencing their Lessons and the negative emotions created in that learning experience.

Now there is this tendency for the human who has experienced one or more challenging existences, and succeeded in healing themselves, to adopt the role of Healer or Teacher in the Earth life. In the Afterlife role, this Soul will use what they have learned in the incarnations on Earth. They will identify themselves as Helper Spirits who interact with their associates on the Earth Plane, and act as Guides, Masters, and so on. This relates well to the concept of the Wounded Healer identity that I speak about in my books.

SETH

Student

The role of student is a popular one for Souls that have recently transitioned from an intense and interesting life. The idea here is that this Soul would benefit from a careful study of the recent life, and perhaps others that are not so recent, to compare and contrast experiences in those lives. Were Lessons learned? What were the Issues that drove behavior in these lives? The student might take many years off of the reincarnational schedule and devote themselves to the study of the life or lives.

The Inner Senses, used through the etheric technology we are calling the Holographic Display, provide for the student researcher deep insights into their own psyche from the recent life. Motivation, emotional content, perceived behavior, all are noted and correlated with outcomes in the created reality.

Teacher

I Seth am a teacher and a philosopher. I am also a Scientist of Consciousness, as I have defined that role for you in my new books. These are my chosen Afterlife vocations, you might say, having lived multiple lives in which I embodied the teacher role, the philosopher role and the explorer of consciousness role. As a teacher I teach others what I

Death and the Afterlife

know, what I know from experience, you see. If you choose this vocation after your Transition, it will be because you have lived similar lives.

Dream State Guide

You may already be providing dream state guidance to others while you are sleeping. This is very common. If you awaken from sleep with the feeling that you were guiding others to dream locations in the Fourth Dimension, it may be that this is quite true. Now again, fantastic, un-believable, yet when you examine what you are doing as you sleep, through experimentation, suggestion, and so on, I believe you may find that Dream State Guide may be only one of the many unbelievable vocations of your Soul Identity.

The Negative Roles

Consciousness does not play favorites in its expression in the physical and non-physical worlds. The opposites of The Virtues of Humanity are realized by consciousness within all dimensions. All probable roles are created by consciousness to be realized in the Afterlife by Soul. This means that a particular Soul may be drawn to any number of obscure, unusual and perhaps negative roles to enact in the non-physical world. Evolutionary Consciousness expresses itself to the nth degree always.

SETH

End of Chapter Experiments

Experiment: Imagine Your Next Life

In this final Experiment of my book, I invite you to use your creative imagination, powered by your Inner Senses, to consider if you will incarnate after your Transition, and if so, what type of existence you might choose.

Now you are aware, more than any other living being, of what your Issues and your Lessons might be. I am guessing that you have given it some thought, perhaps as you have perused this book of mine. With the insights that you have gained on what type of person you are, consider what you may have in store for yourself should you choose another life. Remember, the next life would necessarily involve the addressing of Issues that were neglected or ignored in your current life. Your next life would see you facing those Issues and learning the Lessons created by those Issues.

Create a Light Trance State

Now when you are in this Light Trance State you are experiencing Simultaneous Time. This means that you are pulled out of linear time and may peek in on your Afterlife existence to see what you may

Death and the Afterlife

be doing there. Are you preparing for another life in the Third Dimension? If so, what does that next life entail, in terms of timeframe, location, gender, Issues and Lessons, and so on. This can be a fun exercise for you as well as an opportunity to examine your true self, and make some much needed adjustments. Do you see? When you feel that you have received the information you requested, slowly come up to surface awareness.

Findings: Document your discoveries around possible future life explorations.

Epilogue

I promised you an unusual and entertaining alternative to the Afterlife accounts portrayed in your religious documents. I trust I have kept my promise in this manuscript. All that I ask of you-the Reader, is to take and internalize what speaks to you personally and leave what may not inspire you as much. This material may be successfully combined with any of your regular spiritual practices. However, I do urge you to take a Love Light and not a solemn and dark approach to this integration. Good Humor, you see. Please enjoy your experimentation with this material.

SETH

Questions and Answers

Mark asks:

Seth when and how shall we begin to write the book?

The answer you already know. Let me remind you, however, of our contract. You have been postponing the Death Book. Now that you are experiencing the deaths of your father and mother, you are feeling the need to find out what I have to say. You are also nearing your own death day by day, as you know. This is not a prognosis. This is a fact for you and your cohorts in the Third Dimension.

Now the Home Dimension exists in what you might call the Fourth Dimension. The Fourth Dimension is familiar to you. You are always there, as you know, even though it looks sometimes as if you are trapped in the physical. The answer, then: You are already receiving on the subtle planes my transmission for the new works. When those transmissions emerge into physical Reality Constructs is up to you. Let me say that your back problems are connected to the deaths of your parents, to this project of ours, to your feelings of Lack and your perceived inabilities to create abundance. I will leave you to figure out my meanings. Good luck. All Is Well.

Thanks Seth.

Jason's Questions Related to Eckankar:

So my questions boil down to this:

1. Since we do create our realities as Seth has told us time and again do these planes really exist and not that it's all just sitting there waiting for us, but perhaps do each of us have our own personal version perhaps, and what of the related sound and colour or light, what significance does this have according to their knowledge?

Yes, the planes or dimensions do exist. However, they are open to infinite interpretation. I do not see associative color. I do see that the Etheric Domain favors soft pastels. The colors are a matter of individual choice. Each investigator of the Unknown Reality goes upon their separate journey of discovery. Yet, you have a history of precedents, so to speak, that are available to you mentally via the Telepathic Network. The precedents have to do with the way others in your collectives have perceived All That Is in their explorations. Judgments are made in meditation and prayer, for example, as to what the researcher is experiencing, based upon this pool of ideas, images and emotive concepts that you inherit from your collectives. The collective here is the Soul Family, the family religion, the greater collectives of nation, and the ultimate collective of humanity. All of these collectives offer answers to the questions of the spiritual seeker from within the collective consciousness.

2. Is there an Ascension process through these planes we go through to become one with All That Is and how much do we need 'Masters,' so to speak, if at all to get us there?

There is an Ascension process and there are planes of existence that you negotiate on your way through Soul Evolution. However, this takes place outside of time, where there is no up or down, or time and space. Ascension may be too loose of a description. Expansion may be a more accurate one. You are expanding your personal consciousness to include everything. Your personal consciousness becomes cosmic consciousness. You do need guidance. For it could very well be that your current life will be your final existence, or perhaps merely one of your early attempts. Thus, it does take study in the phys-

Death and the Afterlife

ical world to see where your Soul may be in this expansion process. The non-physical beings help you in this research project. They are your research assistants in the etheric domain. They can guide you to the most successful living experience in your current life to further the evolution of your Soul. This is an old story. Through reading inspirational spiritual literature, the student is motivated to consider what they are doing in the physical world. If they are lucky, they connect with a non-physical Master through the text. They are often asked to identify their Issues and learn their Lessons. This assists the student in achieving Soul Evolution. However, the object is not to become one with All That Is, but to experience your personal Issues and learn your personal Lessons thoroughly in human form in your current existence as this envoy of the Primary Creative Gestalt.

Does the student need Masters at all?

Yes, the student needs their particular Master. For as I have suggested at many points in this manuscript; the God, the Goddess, the Master, the Angel is a collaborative construct of you-the-reader in concert with the creative energies of All That Is. At its base, the Master is you. The Master is you, after you have mastered the earth plane.

SETH

Deon asks from Facebook:

When I had an out of body experience, my Aunt appeared to me and tried to talk me into going over the veil of light. That's the best way I can describe it. My Aunt was in a rest home at the time and not dead. She said, "Come on with me and we will have fun. Grandpa is over there waiting for us." Can you describe for me what was going on? Has this happened to many?

Yes, let me answer your question. Now on your side, you experienced a bleedthrough into the Fourth Dimension. What was going on was this... Your aunt was placing some of her energy into her Home Dimension. This is quite common for the Soul who will soon make the Transition to the Etheric Domain. The physical vehicle is worn out. It ceases to function adequately. The focus becomes one of looking within rather than looking to the outside world. The Inner Senses predominate. The physical senses are relinquished. As your aunt tested the waters, so to speak, of her Home Dimension, she was met by Soul Family members who have already made that journey. The ancestors, the Soul Family members from the current and previous existences, primarily, are there to provide a familiar

Death and the Afterlife

face, to ease anxiety, to lessen the debilitating fear of death. The Soul often takes its time in vacating the physical vehicle. It takes it's time as the Ego/Intellect moves into and adapts to the new reality, in which it is not called upon to create personas that are agreeable to others. The youthful identity has come forward. The life review is in process, here. This is very, very common.

Shelton in Italy asks:

My first Question regarding death and the afterlife..... From my transition dream that I had and Seth responded to I know that there is a point after transitioning you will be met by a guide but how soon after that will you come into contact with your over soul? Seth also told me that there is a "conferencing" with all of your other lives as well, how soon after will the conferencing begin after transitioning? In the home dimension or before in the astral planes?

My third question:

At what stage after transitioning will you begin your life's review? You can re-experience any part of the past life to change things around for learning, Therefore, is it a

SETH

holographic procedure? Also, are your past lives "displayed" holographically for all to see when stationed in the home dimension? How does that work?

Yes, let me unpack your questions. Now first, Shelton, because you are still in the physical, you are obsessed with time. The concept of linear time drives your every waking moment. This is how many of you necessarily construct your lives, around this idea of one moment following the other moment. Now in the non-physical world, **there is no time**. There exists only the spacious moment, the eternal moment of NOW. When you are meditating and you are getting some positive effects, you are in the NOW. When you have a momentary awakening of ecstasy, and you remember your power, you are in the NOW moment. When you have these moments of contact with your Higher Centers of Awareness, please note, that, you experience a time<u>less</u> reality. In the timeless NOW moment, there is no such thing as sequence or location.

After your physical death, and I am talking to you personally, you will experience your expectations. These expectations are built around various aspects of my Teaching and some beliefs that you have valued enough to keep over the years. Yes,

Death and the Afterlife

your Guide will meet you. This will be a construct created around who you think I am. Your Simultaneous Lives will all be apparent to you. In their totality, you will know them intimately, for you are they, you see. You have a desire to witness the Holographic Display, and return to some pleasant experiences from your past, and so you will do that. Your main goal, however, is to return for one last life, in order to grasp more firmly some of the spiritual truths you are uncovering in this life.

Now when do these etheric events transpire? For you I see these events as occurring in a split second. You are eager to return, you see. Even though you have just arrived in the Home Dimension, you are like this eager student, ready for another assignment. I do see you returning to an earlier era, however. You will most likely choose to incarnate during the Renaissance in what is now Europe. This is entirely possible for you.

Carol Joy asks:

Dear Seth, there seems to be two kinds of people in terms of having an ability to connect with loved ones who have died. One group instinctively knows how to do this; the other group finds it impossible. Are

there exercises to help someone give themselves permission to interact with deceased relatives, lovers or friends? If so, please describe these exercises.

Yes, there are two types of people with regards to having the communication skills necessary to speak to friends and family members who are in the Home Dimension. I have offered some experiments for my students who have difficulties in making that initial contact. A simple method you may use to contact loved ones who have passed on, is to, in a manner of speaking, **pretend** that you are making contact. This comes first. The perception of contact. Now I have said before in my books and lectures that the Ancestors, loved ones and friends who are transitioned, do indeed wish to connect with you also. At various points in this book I have suggested that maintaining contact with the Third Dimension and the people in it is of great importance to the Afterlife inhabitants. So pretending, visualizing, acting as if you are in contact already, takes the anxiety out of the equation. You are simply playing a game, you see. You are not conjuring ghosts. You are utilizing your creative imagination as you did when you were a child communicating with people from your Past Lives and talking to your imaginary playmates. Acting as if, makes it a harmless endeavor;

Death and the Afterlife

child's play. Your cynical side stays out of the picture, here, for you are re-experiencing your Magical Child aspect of consciousness. There is no room for cynicism and fear in this perspective. Additionally, you WILL get results. I can assure you of that at this time. When you receive the response from the loved one in question, please give thanks. Be grateful for the gesture of their penetrating the dimensional veils. Be grateful and joyous. Ask some questions. Remember the answers you receive and write them down after the session. Make an appointment to speak in the very near future. Then keep that appointment, as though it were the very important responsibility that it indeed is. This is how it is done.

Ritual of Sanctuary

The Ritual of Sanctuary was presented to readers in our book on **Soul Evolution** when we first began to emphasize direct exploration of the Unknown Reality. We felt that the reader would require some personalized protection in their experimentation.

The most simple form of the Ritual is to imagine, prior to psychic pursuits, a golden Light surrounding you. Nothing harmful can penetrate this field of Light. It has a healing protective influence. You may certainly use this simplified form while you go about creating your own Ritual.

The object here is to generate positive energies with your creative consciousness. Try listing on a piece of paper your positive beliefs and ideas that denote security, peace, and protection. The next step would be, perhaps artistically, to distill these potent concepts down into an image, statement, or physical object that Resonates with the protective energies. Naturally you may include gestures, visualizations, or any other evocative materials.

SETH

Practice your Ritual until you can create at-will the state of Sanctuary within your own consciousness. Only you will know when you are successful.

Glossary

Definitions for the concepts Seth discusses in this book.

All That Is - The energy source from which all life sprung throughout the multitude of Universes, transcending all dimensions of consciousness and being part of all. Also referred to as the Logos and Evolutionary Consciousness.

Altared States - Ritualizing and making sacred the mundane activities of existence creates elevated states of consciousness.

Ancient Wisdom - The knowledge of the magicians, shamans, witches and healers of the past.

Appreciation - Profound comprehension with Loving Understanding. A thorough expression of gratitude and humility for what you are experiencing and creating.

Awakening - As the Ancient Wisdom is remembered by humanity, an awareness of the greater reality is experienced by individuals.

Back Engineering - the momentary practice of selecting from the current Reality Creation those elements that represent the Best Case Scenario.

Beliefs - Ideas, images, and emotions within your mental environment that act as filters and norms in the creation of Personal Realities.

Best Case Scenario - The ideal outcome for your Reality Creation Project exists in the Probable Future within the Pre-manifestation Domain.

Bleedthroughs - Momentary experiencing of lives

SETH

being lived in other timeframes and other systems of reality.

Catharsis - Recovering lost aspects of the Essential Identity.

Co-creation - You co-create your reality with the limitless creative energies of All That Is.

Common Trance - The consciousness of the status quo collective. Supports consumerism and blind obedience to authority.

Consciousness Units (CU's) - The theorized building blocks of realities. Elements of awarized energy that are telepathic and holographic.

Consecutive Positive Assessments (CPA's) - A technique of positive Reality Creation, in which the student finds something positive, something worthwhile in each experience in physical reality.

Courage - Courage and Loving Understanding replace fear and anger in the creation of Positive Realities.

Denial - The ego/intellect prevents the learning of Lessons by denying the truth of the matter.

Dimensions - Points of reference from one reality to the other with different vibrational wavelengths of consciousness.

Divine Day - The student attempts to live a complete waking day while maintaining contact with the Energy Personality.

Divine Will - The will is potentiated through ongoing contact and communication with Beings of Light. Also called Intent.

Ego/Intellect - The aspect of the personality that

attempts to maintain the status quo reality.

Ecstasy - The positive emotion experienced in contact with the Divine.

Embodiment - Precepts are lived in the creation of improved realities.

Emotional Body - An Inner Senses representation of your current expression in physical reality.

Energy Personality - A being capable of transferring their thought energy inter-dimensionally to physical beings and sometimes using the physical abilities of those beings for communication.

Entity - Being not presently manifested on the physical plane. Also known as a Spirit.

Essential Identity - A truthful representation of the personality as perceived with the Inner Senses.

Feeling-Tone - Thoughts, images, sounds and assorted sensory data that represent a particular state of consciousness, event, or existence.

Fourth-Dimensional Shift - Consciousness expands as the individual experiences an awareness of all Simultaneous Existences. Also called Unity of Consciousness Awareness.

Frequency - Each human being, each blade of grass, each grain of sand vibrates at a particular frequency.

Gestalts of Consciousness - Assemblages of Consciousness Units into Reality Constructs of all types.

gods - Consciousness personalized and projected outward into reality. A self-created projection of the developing ego. See non-physical beings.

Holographic Insert - Teaching aid of the non-physical beings. Multisensory construct experienced with the Inner Senses.

Higher Centers of Awareness - See Energy Personality, Entity and Objective Observer Perspective.

Home Dimension - Home to your Etheric Body after you make your Transition and in between your lives.

Incarnation - To move oneself into another life experience on the physical plane.

Inner Sense - The Soul's perspective. Both the creator and the perceiver of Personal Realities.

Instant Manifestation - In the New Consciousness, there is the potential to experience no lag time in the creation of realities.

Intellectualization - The aspect of the psyche that attempts to figure things out so that the status quo is maintained.

Intention - See Divine Will.

IIssues - Your personality aspects that bring you into conflict with others and create negative emotion.

Lessons - Chosen life experiences of the Soul for further spiritual evolution.

Light Body - The etheric body of refined light.

Love - Love with a capital L is the force behind manifestation in the Third Dimension.

Death and the Afterlife

Magical Child - The perspective of the researcher that allows for experiencing and creating the existence through the eyes of of the magical, empowered, pre-socialized identity.

Metaphorical Tool - An empowered visualized construct that the researcher uses to explore the physical and the non-physical worlds.

Moment Point - The current empowered moment of awakening. Exists as a portal to all points past, present and future and all Simultaneous Lives.

Multitasking - To function consciously in both the physical Third Dimension and the metaphysical Fourth, Fifth and Sixth Dimensions.

Mystery Civilizations - Foundational civilizations largely unknown to modern science. Some examples are Atlantis, Lemuria and GA.

Negative Emotion - Habitual creation of negative emotions creates enduring negative realities.

Negative Entities - Negative energies that roam the Universes in pursuit of their own power to dominate.

Negative Persona - Rejected and repressed aspects of the personal identity.

Negative Reality - See Negative Emotion.

New Consciousness - Multi-Dimensional Consciousness is available to those who are exploring the Third Dimension with the help of their non-physical Guides.

Nonphysical Beings - By focusing on All That Is, you help to identify and create your Guides, Helpers, Fairies, Angels and so on.

Objective Observer Perspective - Self-created aspect of consciousness that sees beyond the limitations of the ego/intellect. An intermediary position between the ego and the Soul Self.

Percept - Perception creates reality in the Third Dimension through the Inner Senses.

Personal Reality Field - The radius within your self created world within which you have the most control in the creation of Reality Constructs.

Point of Power - The current empowered Moment Point allows the practitioner to make changes within past, present or future lives.

Precept - Empowered concepts of manifestation. Example: you create your own reality.

Pre-Manifestation Domain - Theorized dimension where all realities exist prior to receiving sufficient energy to emerge into the Third Dimension.

Reality - That which one assumes to be true based on one's thoughts and experiences. Also called Perceived Reality.

Reality Creation - Consciousness creates reality.

Reincarnational Drama - Soul Family drama enacted to teach the participants a Lesson in Value Fulfillment.

Resonance - Within the Telepathic Network, CU's assemble, separate and reassemble according to frequency.

Scientist of Consciousness - The researcher studies the phenomena within the Personal Reality Field by testing hypotheses in experimentation. See Precept.

Seth - An energy personality essence that has appeared within the mental environments of humans throughout the millennia to educate and inspire.

Simultaneous Lives - The multidimensional simultaneous experiences of Souls in incarnation.

Simultaneous Time - Everything that can happen does happen in the current timeless moment of creation.

Soul - The non-physical counterpart to the physical human body, the personality, and the mentality. The spiritual aspect of the human.

Soul Evolution - The conscious learning of Lessons without denial or intellectualization.

Soul Family - The group of humans you incarnate with lifetime after lifetime to learn your Lessons together.

Soul Mates - Loving mates who are awakening together.

Spiritual Hierarchy - Beings of Light who have mastered multidimensional levels of experience throughout the Universes and have moved on to higher service in the evolution of all Souls.

Subconscious Projection - Most of your reality is created subconsciously as you project the contents of your subconscious mind into the Third Dimension.

Subtext - The unspoken truth of a statement that is sensed intuitively. It can come in a burst of intuition, or quite subtly as in a growing understanding.

The Christ - The embodiment of The Christ in your

World. Also called World Teacher. First described in Seth Speaks.

The Council - Members of the Spiritual Hierarchy. Highly evolved beings that advise Souls on incarnations for their spiritual evolution.

The New World - The Positive Manifestation

The Vanguard - Advocates for humanity and Mother Earth who incarnate together to lead progressive movements of various kinds.

Third Dimension - The physical plane of Earthly existence.

Trance State - The relaxed, focused state of awareness that allows the Scientist of Consciousness to conduct experiments and collect data.

Trust but Verify - You take on faith the material from your Higher Centers of Awareness and you continually verify to confirm this information.

Uncommon Trance - This altared state honors the integrity and authority of the individual. You are inner-directed and naturally abide by the suggestions of your Higher Centers of Awareness.

Value Fulfillment - Consciousness seeks manifestation of itself into all realities via the fulfillment of all values.

Visionary - Reincarnated magicians, shamans, witches and healers in this current timeframe.

Vision Statement - The Visionary creates an empowered oath or proclamation that will guide their efforts in the Reality Creation Project.

When You Walk Across the Room

Dear Reader, when you walk across the room, you are with each movement forward, re-creating your physical body according to your essential identity out of the Consciousness Units that exist as air in front of you; space, you see. It is not a matter of "bringing" your body across the room, it is more a case of re-creating your body in its totality within this field - within this medium, if you prefer - of holographic units of awarized energy: the Consciousness Units.

Step-by-step, then, your sacred identity - this Soul Self - assembles the physical body of you-the-reader from the CUs "in front of it." The CUs - identified as atoms, or molecules, or CUs of air - are transformed into CUs of blood, flesh, and bone.

Now... in the same precise fashion, the birds as they swoop down to feed, are creating from the CUs of air before them, their bird bodies.

But what of the tree, the mountain, you might ask? As the tree sways in the wind, it re-creates itself out of the CUs of earth and air surrounding it. As the mountain endures the weathering forces of rain and wind, it retains its mountain identity and re-creates itself with minute or catastrophic alterations, according to this weathering over time.

9 780974 058658